At last! Newton's Attachment Connection *takes attachment and neuroscience into the mainstream of parenting and clinical practice, bringing clarity and insight to the often misunderstood world of family bonds. Using a sensitive combination of informative vignettes, lucid explanations, and developmental milestones, she deftly illuminates the nature of the bond that develops between parents and their babies and the profound influence which this bond will have on a baby's ability to form secure attachments. As a therapist and academic, Newton's comprehensive knowledge of the socio-emotional development of children shines through with intelligence, passion, humor, and sensitivity.*

> —Sir Richard Bowlby Bt., president of the Centre for Child Mental Health in London, UK

Drawing on the latest scientific research and her extensive clinical experience, Newton has written a practical guide for parents who seek to foster an attachment bond with their young children (infants through three years of age). Since a secure attachment forms the foundation for children's later social and emotional development, this is must read book for parents.

> —Charles E. Schaefer, Ph.D., professor of psychology at Fairleigh Dickinson University in Teaneck, NJ, and cofounder and director emeritus of the Association for Play Therapy

"[Ruth Newton] has written a valuable book..."

> —Library Journal

THE
ATTACHMENT CONNECTION

Parenting a Secure
& Confident Child
Using the Science of
Attachment Theory

RUTH P. NEWTON, PH.D.

New Harbinger Publications, Inc.

Publisher's Note

Distributed in Canada by Raincoast Books

Copyright © 2008 by Ruth P. Newton
New Harbinger Publications, Inc.
5674 Shattuck Avenue
Oakland, CA 94609
www.newharbinger.com

Acquired by Tesilya Hanauer; Cover design by Amy Shoup;
Edited by Brady Kahn

Library of Congress Cataloging-in-Publication Data
Newton, Ruth P.
  The attachment connection : parenting a secure and confident child using the science of attachment theory / Ruth P. Newton.
     p. cm.
  ISBN-13: 978-1-57224-520-4 (pbk. : alk. paper)
  ISBN-10: 1-57224-520-4 (pbk. : alk. paper) 1. Attachment behavior. I. Title.
  BF723.A75N49 2008
  155.6'46--dc22
                              2008011920

15 14 13

10 9 8 7 6 5 4 3

To all children born longing to feel known

Contents

FOREWORD   xi

ACKNOWLEDGMENTS   xv

INTRODUCTION   1

A Paradigm Shift: Increasing the Focus on Your Child's
    Emotional Development

Purpose of This Book

Definition of Terms

CHAPTER 1: **Attachment Matters**   7

Setting the Scene: Reconnecting with the Natural
    Instinct for Attachment

Attachment Defined

The History of Attachment Theory

Organized Attachment Styles

Disorganized Attachment

Comparing Organized and Disorganized Attachment

Internal Working Models: We All Have Early Childhood
    Experiences

Attachment Categories over Time

What Secure Children Learn

What Insecure-Avoidant and -Ambivalent Children Learn

What Disorganized Children Learn

Temperament and Attachment

You Don't Have to Parent the Way You Were Parented

Parents Need to Be Good Enough, Not Perfect

In a Nutshell: Attachment Security Is Built with Parental
    Attunement and Sensitivity

CHAPTER 2: **What's Behind the Face**   35
Setting the Scene: Visualizing the Interior World of the Brain
Entrainment: Synchronizing Two Systems
Shaping Your Baby's Brain
Two Brains Meet: Nonverbal Communication Between
    You and Your Baby
Shifting to the Right: Making Time to Tune In to Your Child
Helping Your Child Pass Through the Survival Gates
Building Regulated Brains: How Parents Help
Emotional Regulation and Dysregulation: Case Examples
Wiring Optimal Arousal Ranges into the Autonomic
    Nervous System
In a Nutshell: Regulate Negative Emotions While Enhancing
    Positive Emotions

CHAPTER 3: **Crossing into a New Ocean:**
Pregnancy, Birth, and the Newborn Period   65
Setting the Scene: The Transition to Parenthood
Marriages, Commitments, and Other Necessary Ingredients
It Really Does Take a Village: Your Support System
Work Absorption: Balancing Home and Work
Building Your Family Infrastructure: Expect Change
Pregnancy
Fetal Movement
Approaching the Birth
The New Ocean: After Your Baby Is Born
The Newborn Period
Keys to Attachment
In a Nutshell: Take Care of Yourselves

CHAPTER 4: **We're Still Breathing!**
The Two-Month-Old   87
Setting the Scene: Jordan's Need for Contact
Developmental Milestones: Building Connection as Your
    Baby Grows

Cultivating Secure Attachment in the Two-Month-Old
Play and Attachment in the Two-Month-Old
Parent Focus: Reentering the Adult World
Living in the Charm: Pippa's Response to Her New
   Three-Month-Old Cousin

CHAPTER 5: **There *Is* Someone in There!**
The Four-Month-Old   99
Setting the Scene: China's Need for Predictable Interactions
Developmental Milestones: Building Connection as Your
   Baby Grows
Cultivating Secure Attachment in the Four-Month-Old
Play and Attachment in the Four-Month-Old
Parent Focus: Celebrations
Living in the Charm: Daniel's Attempt to Help

CHAPTER 6: **Knowing the Clan:**
The Six-Month-Old   111
Setting the Scene: Corey and His Young Mother
Developmental Milestones: Building Connection as Your
   Baby Grows
Cultivating Secure Attachment in the Six-Month-Old
Play and Attachment in the Six-Month-Old
Parent Focus: A Night Off
Living in the Charm: Randy's Gift from Heaven

CHAPTER 7: **There's a Stranger Amongst Us!**
The Nine-Month-Old   123
Setting the Scene: Amy's Struggle for Exploration
Developmental Milestones: Building Connection as Your
   Baby Grows
Cultivating Secure Attachment in the Nine-Month-Old
Play and Attachment in the Nine-Month-Old
Parent Focus: Family Vacations
Living in the Charm: Kara Finds Her Beat!

CHAPTER 8: **Free at Last: The Twelve-Month-Old**　　137

Setting the Scene: Max's Attempts to Take Care of His Mother

Developmental Milestones: Building Connection as Your
Baby Grows

Cultivating Secure Attachment in the Twelve-Month-Old

Play and Attachment in the Twelve-Month-Old

Parent Focus: A Day at the Amusement Park

Living in the Charm: August's Social Protocol

CHAPTER 9: **I Think, Therefore I Am:**
The Eighteen-Month-Old　　149

Setting the Scene: Morgan's Terror

Developmental Milestones: Building Connection as Your
Toddler Grows

Cultivating Secure Attachment in the Eighteen-Month-Old

Play and Attachment in the Eighteen-Month-Old

Parent Focus: A Single Dad at Play

Living in the Charm: Owen's Learning How to Count

CHAPTER 10: **Where Did He Hear That Word?**
The Two-Year-Old　　163

Setting the Scene: Cohen's Struggle with His Mother

Developmental Milestones: Building Connection as Your
Toddler Grows

Cultivating Secure Attachment in the Two-Year-Old

Play and Attachment in the Two-Year-Old

Parent Focus: A Day at the Spa

Living in the Charm: Tess's Push Back

CHAPTER 11: **Shifting to the Left:**
The Three-Year-Old　　177

Setting the Scene: Kierra's Working for Attention

Developmental Milestones: Building Connection as Your
Preschooler Grows

Cultivating Secure Attachment in the Three-Year-Old

Play and Attachment in the Three-Year-Old

Parent Focus: Floor Time for Dad

Living in the Charm: Valerie's Perplexity

CHAPTER 12: **I Can Do It Myself:**
The Four-Year-Old   191
    Setting the Scene: Dennis's Need for Unstructured Time
    Developmental Milestones: Building Connection as Your
      Preschooler Grows
    Cultivating Secure Attachment in the Four-Year-Old
    Play and Attachment in the Four-Year-Old
    Parent Focus: Health-Conscious Parents
    Living in the Charm: Jack's Curiosity

CHAPTER 13: **Baby on the Go**   203
    Child Care Research
    Quality of Child Care
    More Options Are Needed
    Family and Medical Leave Act
    In Parting: Attachment Matters

References   213

Foreword

In the midst of our busy day-to-day lives the broadcast and written media continuously inform us that scientific information is increasing at an extremely rapid rate. Perhaps the most publicized of these advances in knowledge are the breakthroughs in brain research reported over the course of and since "the decade of the brain." Indeed these exciting discoveries in neuroscience are now generating more complex understandings of certain fundamental problems of the human condition. One such problem is the question of early human development—why are the beginning stages of life so critical to every aspect of an individual's functioning over the entire life span? A large body of biological and psychological studies are now exploring the precise mechanisms by which nature and nurture interact in order to shape a unique personality. These studies are giving us much deeper and practically useful models of the early origins of both adaptive resilience as well as vulnerabilities of later mental health.

As a result of this surge of new information about development our scientific understanding of human infancy is now undergoing a profound change. Until recently the focus was on cognitive and physical development, that is on the early stages of the baby's thinking and the precursors of language. In contrast, all current disciplines studying infancy are now focusing on the centrality of early social and emotional development. These investigators are looking beyond just outer behavior and into the early relational development of the baby's inner mind, and exploring how this mind, before the appearance of language, communicates its emotional states to another mind. Developmental psychologists, psychiatrists, and neuroscientists are all converging on the critical role that emotional development, even more than intellect, plays on later mental and physical well being. Thus, it is now thought that the essential tasks of human infancy are the formation of an attachment bond of emotional communication between infant and mother, the expansion of the child's capacity to experience and communicate positive and negative emotions (affects), and the emergence of the ability to use others and self to regulate these emotions.

Neuroscience now demonstrates that the critical period of emotional and social development of infancy occurs during the brain growth spurt. More than any other stage of life the last trimester of pregnancy through the second year represents the period of most rapid and maximal brain growth of axons, dendrites, synapses, and myelin. The principle that nature's potential can only be realized as it is enabled by nurture reflects the fact that this tremendous expansion of brain growth is experience-dependent, and that these essential early experiences are provided in the emotional communications of the attachment relationship between the infant and primary caregiver. It is now established that the emotion processing right brain develops in the first year, before the language processing left in the second year. Thus the evolutionary purpose of the child's forming an attachment bond with the mother is more than just to transmit psychological experiences. Rather, at the most fundamental level, attachment experiences with a sensitive primary caregiver promote brain development, specifically of the right brain, which for the rest of the life span is dominant for emotional functions, nonverbal communication, the regulation of bodily states, stress, empathy, intuition, and indeed survival.

Although this information is now deeply penetrating psychology, psychiatry, social work, and pediatrics, the larger meaning of this research for parents has not yet been sufficiently addressed. In this remarkable book, Ruth Newton, a skilled infant psychologist with both a substantial knowledge of normal and abnormal early development and of attachment theory and early brain development, effectively and creatively translates the practical aspects of these recent advances in the science of human infancy to the matter of early childrearing. Newton is in a unique position to write this book. Her work as psychology supervisor of Child and Family Mental Health Services at St. Vincent de Paul Village in San Diego has given her in depth access to hundreds of cases of mother-infant psychotherapy. There are far fewer experts that work with children than adults, and psychologists with clinical experiences with infants and toddlers are even rarer. In addition, her studies with me in developmental affective neuroscience give her a deep knowledge of early right brain development, and a valuable wide-ranging interdisciplinary perspective of both the psychology and neuropsychology of early emotional development. She possesses a gift for not only being able to present a very extensive body of current scientific information, but also the ability to organize this information about the baby's right brain and inner world in clear and comprehensible language. In light of the fact that parent-infant communication is fundamentally nonverbal communication, this book is a valuable primer on the unique functions of the right brain.

Indeed, Newton has produced a volume as informative to parents as earlier volumes by Spock and Brazelton. But unlike other books in the field, here the focus is on modern relational models of infancy, on emotions, and on brain development. She shows a talent for not only identifying and describing the operations of complex brain mechanisms into identifiable familiar day-to-day interactions, but also for sketching very personal portraits of a variety of different patterns of modern families: working parents, blended families, single caregivers, the role of grandparents, and stay at home moms/dads. Although there now exists a diversity of family structures, all human infants are born with a survival motivation to attach to a primary caregiver in order to homeostatically regulate their bodily-based biological functions and to optimize brain development. In addition to individual chapters on all stages of brain development and emerging social-emotional functions, in the last chapter Newton offers an informative and provocative evaluation of current childcare from the perspective of affective neuroscience.

The Attachment Connection focuses on the social-emotional experiences that optimize the development of the infant's right brain, mind, and body. The right brain undergoes an "experience-dependent maturation" in the first two years, and its neurobiological development is more than just genetically encoded. Interpersonal neurobiology clearly demonstrates that right brain maturation is impacted, for better or worse, by relational experiences. The technical term "enriched environment" has been used in science mostly in terms of altering the infant's physical environment in order to facilitate the child's verbal language skills and voluntary behavior. But now this concept is being used to describe an enriched social environment, one which optimizes right brain growth and complexity. As Newton shows, this scientific principle has direct relevance to more complex models of parenting.

By portraying infants as right brain emotional and social beings more so than left-brain developing thinking machines, Newton creates true three- dimensional portraits of young children who are developing iden-tifiable unique personalities. Indeed, a major discovery of current infant studies is that the essential processes of personality, organizing relation-ships and regulating interpersonal stress, emerge pre- and postnatally, during the brain growth spurt, and not later when the child acquires language capacities. Throughout the life span not just verbal intelligence but social intelligence is necessary for the optimal functioning of a per-sonality. All thoughtful parents are aware that, at a conscious and an unconscious level, they profoundly influence the development of their child's personality. Science now clearly indicates that this impact is most profound during the brain growth spurt in the first years of life. This important book on the neurobiological effects of parenting is essential reading for all psychologically minded parents.

—Allan N. Schore, Ph.D.
UCLA David Geffen School of Medicine
Author of *Affect Regulation and the Origin of the Self* and
Affect Dysregulation and Disorders of the Self

Acknowledgments

The excellent thought of many attachment researchers has informed my thinking for a number of years, but none more so than the work of Allan Schore. With the publication of his 1994 book came a base for understanding what a clinical developmental psychologist experiences on a daily basis. It permanently changed my perspective, allowing me to deeply integrate what I see in the developing child into a theory that guides intervention. I could not have written this book without the ongoing exposure to Allan Schore's thought and support and the stimulating interactions with my colleagues in the Schore Los Angeles study group. I want to personally thank Allan and Judy Schore for their commitment.

My two-week training with Alan Sroufe, June Sroufe, and Betty Carlson at the Institute of Child Development in Minnesota, where I learned to rate the attachment categories from Strange Situation videos, continues to be a lovely memory to which I return often in my mind. Not only have these researchers greatly contributed to the field of attachment, but their compassion, humor, and humanity is palpable, leaving those of us who were fortunate enough to have been trained by them with a model of a researcher walking hand in hand with life.

Another experience that has greatly affected my thinking was my work with Sonia Gojman de Millan, Nancy Kaplan, Mary Main, and Erik Hesse on the Adult Attachment Interview (AAI). Knowing that a parent's state of mind with respect to attachment can predict a child's attachment category has made me more conscious of the language adults use to describe their early experiences. My thanks, in particular, to Mary and Erik, who not only gave an excellent training workshop on the AAI in Los Angeles but did so with grace, humor, and sensitive responsiveness to those of us fortunate to attend.

My thanks to the residents and staff of St. Vincent de Paul Village, who have supported our work with children age birth to five and their families. I want to especially thank my colleagues Bill Matulich, Gil Gentile, and Joanna Hirst for their ongoing support. My deep admiration and appreciation goes to the staff members at SAY San Diego's Extended Day child care program, who have allowed me to serve as their consultant for many years, and particularly to Susan "Starshine" Sharkey for her ongoing commitment to the "Starshine Hour." Thanks also goes to the numerous graduate students, particularly Kelly Baier, Alicia Farrell, and Heather Chamberlain, who have contributed to the ongoing work at St. Vincent's. I am especially grateful to my administrative assistant, Connie Mullan, who also serves as the coordinator for the birth-to-five program and keeps us afloat. I also want to thank the adults, children, and families who have shared their lives with me in private practice.

This book would not have been written had it not been for Matt McKay, cofounder of New Harbinger Publications, approaching me after a talk that I gave in the Schore developmental panel at the California Psychological Association convention. Thank you, Matt. My thanks to Tesilya Hanauer, acquisitions manager at New Harbinger, for her ongoing support and quick response throughout the process, and a special thanks to Brady Kahn for her excellent editing, which has greatly improved the book; she is also the first mother of a child under five to have read the book in its entirety.

There are many people in my personal life who have encouraged me to write. A special thanks to my writing group, Maggie Barker, Pat Dean, and Kathleen Durning, who tolerated my absence from meetings so that I could write! Also thanks to Rick Avery, Mallory Landers, Gita Morena, Trish Stanley, and my family, both past and present, for their ongoing support over many years, and especially to Jill Weckerly, who read the first four chapters and gave me much encouragement to continue.

Introduction

You may have heard about attachment theory, which is increasingly in the public's consciousness. Yet you may not know how the quality of your child's attachment to you is intricately linked to his brain development and emotional regulation. In the past, the field of child development focused less on the complex and mostly nonverbal world of social-emotional development and more on the growth of cognitive and motor skills because these skills were relatively easy to see and thus measure. The connection between emotions and behavior was even more problematic to measure because of its tighter coupling with the child's unique environmental experience.

This all changed when John Bowlby wrote his trilogy on attachment suggesting that a child's attachment to his parent was a biological system that served to protect the child (Bowlby 1969/1982, 1973, 1980) and that this system could significantly be altered based upon the quality of the parent's response to the child's need to attach (Ainsworth et al. 1978). The thought that parenting could affect a biological system spurred an enormous amount of research focused on the dyadic nature, that is, the "twoness," of parent-child interactions that characterizes social-emotional development. As neuroscience began to provide more evidence for how the brain functions and develops, especially identifying critical growth periods within the first few years of life, the social-emotional domain of development began to come out of the shadows to stand squarely on the shoulders of the child's attachment to his parents. Now, not only can the quality of a child's attachment to his caregivers be determined, but many studies have shown what it means to a child's ongoing development. In fact, studies that have followed infants through childhood and into adulthood are consistently showing that the quality of the early parent-child relationship appears to directly affect a child's emotional security, his sense of self, and even his cognitive development (Sroufe et al. 2005).

A PARADIGM SHIFT: INCREASING THE FOCUS ON YOUR CHILD'S EMOTIONAL DEVELOPMENT

We are currently in the throes of a paradigm shift away from an almost exclusive focus on the mind and its cognitive skills, back toward the importance of emotions, feelings, and body communications. An impetus for this shift occurred in 1994 with the publication of a book by Allan Schore, entitled *Affect Regulation and the Origin of the Self*. Citing over 2,000 references, Schore integrated psychological, psychoanalytical, and developmental theories with current infant and brain research. In brief, he concluded that the attachment process was intrinsic to brain development and, in particular, to the maturation of the right hemisphere. According to Schore, caregiver-infant interactions are the primary force involved in regulating an infant's internal physiology and the structural development of the brain. This means that the quality of your child's attachment to you corresponds to how emotionally regulated your child's internal physiology will be, which, in turn, corresponds to the health of your child's brain development. Helping your child regulate his internal physiology allows him to use his whole brain and all of its gifts to authentically learn, explore, and express.

The impact of attachment and affect regulation theories has profoundly changed our understanding of the importance of emotional development. Instead of tacking on social-emotional development as the third domain, trailing after cognitive and motor domains, when assessing a child's development, it must be seen as the primary developmental domain upon which all future development rests.

The social-emotional development of a child, then, has much to do with sensitive and attuned caregiver-child interactions, for these interactions not only create feelings of security for the child but also regulate his autonomic nervous system so that important regulatory centers in the brain develop and mature. It is now increasingly accepted that chronic problems in early childhood, such as parental abuse and neglect, domestic violence, loss of caregivers, and severe parental depression and/or anxiety, can affect this process, thereby leaving the child with a dysregulated nervous system and incomplete structural development in the brain (Schore 2003).

This may seem like a heavy responsibility for you, as a parent, but I have written this book to help you raise secure children using what is known about attachment and affect regulation. As a long-practicing clinician who uses these two theories in my work with adults, families, and children, I present this important information using real family examples. You will also learn that attunement to your child doesn't entail a dogmatic list of must-dos. In fact, *good enough* parenting means that you are providing enough attunement to your child's needs for him to trust that he can rely on you for help if needed, that you can understand and protect him, and that you can help him regulate his emotions until he is able to regulate his own. Attunement is how this is done, and I will talk throughout the book about how attuned enough parents provide a secure base for their young child.

Affective neuroscience is the study of the underlying brain processes, neural systems, and organization involved in emotions, feelings, and instinctual responses. It is assumed that instinct plays a pivotal role in human survival and evolution. The affective neuroscientist Jaak Panksepp (1998) points out the similarity between the emotion centers in the human brain and that of many animals, thereby anchoring in evolution the fundamental link of emotions and feelings to behavior. Too often, feelings and instincts are ignored in favor of conceptual thought, yet it is only with feelings and instinct that babies can initially express themselves. Although we cannot directly know the interior world of another person, through our own feelings, we are able to match someone else's feelings. This is called *empathy*. The possession of empathy, humor, good judgment, compassion, creativity, insight, and positive values, along with the ability to regulate his emotions, will not only help your child express himself but will also contribute to a more civilized world. All of these human capabilities are associated with attunement and the development of the right cerebral hemisphere, the hemisphere that houses the deepest connections to our bodies and instincts.

Empathy - ability to match someone else's feelings.

PURPOSE OF THIS BOOK

This book is about the importance of the early parent-child relationship, how it affects brain development, and how good enough parenting leads to secure attachment and emotionally regulated children. Early attachment plays a huge role in the healthy development of your child's social-emotional skills. To increase awareness of the links between parenting and social-emotional development, this book has been specifically written to bring attachment and affect regulation theories, along with the impressive research that supports them, to parents, child care staff, and those involved with the care of children under the age of five. It is my desire to strengthen your understanding of the "body world," the important nonverbal world of body communications that some may have forgotten. It is this world that is involved in responding sensitively to your infant, and it is this language that your baby speaks.

DEFINITION OF TERMS

Because of the complexity involved in understanding the brain, the field of neuroscience has attempted to develop a common language. This language may be unfamiliar to parents. Since affective neuroscience does appear to be the vanguard force, which is already making a profound change in our understanding of human development, it will be important for parents who are interested in attachment theory to have some familiarity with common terms.

Affect regulation or *emotional regulation* is the ability to modulate your positive and negative emotions. For example, an adult faced with a boss who is critical may feel anger, disappointment, frustration, stress, and hurt, but he can modulate these intense feelings given the situation and choose an appropriate response, such as evaluating and talking with his boss about realistic expectations. Affect regulation implies the ability to keep your own nervous system within optimal ranges.

Affect dysregulation describes emotional states that are outside the range of what we consider normal for the event or situation. Using the same example, an adult who does not have affect regulation may become emotionally reactive and angrily confront his boss and use a few choice words before walking out of the workplace in a huff. This is affect dysregulation: the adult does not have control over his emotions and therefore cannot entertain an appropriate response; nor can he keep his own nervous system within an optimal range. All too often, these emotional regulation problems in adulthood are etched into the brain early on. You will learn how your attunement to your child's interior world of feeling has everything to do with the quality of his attachment to you, which has everything to do with his emotional regulation, which in turn allows him to freely learn and explore.

Most parents will naturally relate to the terms *emotions* and *feelings*, which I use more often than the term *affect* in the text. However, all three terms refer to a child's interior and/or exterior states of sensation, feeling, and emotion, whether seen or unseen by the parent, and include the corresponding neural changes in the child's brain. There will be other terms presented within the chapters, along with examples, to aid you in understanding attachment and affect regulation theories and their importance to your child's future. In general, however, I have attempted to select the most commonly heard term associated with a particular parent-child experience. Figure 1 in chapter 2 shows the important brain sites associated with attachment and development.

Because attunement has everything to do with your own right brain, this book includes scenes with enough imagery to hopefully pull you into your own "right minds" as you read along. I also use the pronoun "we" to indicate that what is talked about in the text applies to all of us. So "you" and "me" and "we" and "us" mean you are not in this alone. Too often, parents who are trying their best are stuck because they have a sense that they are supposed to know how to parent automatically, as if nature has encoded some kind of a "Guide to Parenting" directly into our genes. Nature did do something like that, but in the form of instincts that, of course, may have been bent a bit by our own upbringings. So I will talk a lot about your support and care.

To reduce confusion on the use of his/her pronouns, I have alternated genders by chapter, but all the material in this book refers to both male and female babies unless I've stated otherwise.

This book gives examples of typical and atypical development in children age birth to five and their families. The first two chapters present what is known about attachment and affect regulation as it affects child development; these chapters are the foundation for understanding your developing child. Chapter 3 covers the period of pregnancy, birth, and the newborn period. The succeeding developmental chapters attempt to approach attachment and affect regulation by developmental age. Chapter 13 provides relevant information to parents who need child care. You can read the book in a number of ways, but if you choose to start with a chapter that matches the age of your child, be sure to read chapters 1 and 2 first.

With these things said, welcome to the world of attachment!

CHAPTER 1

Attachment Matters

*Who would have guessed that within minutes
of his birth, I would give my life to protect
seven pounds of flesh.*
—a new father

Raising secure, emotionally competent, cooperative children who have full access to their creativity and expression is desperately needed for the health of the human race and the health of the planet. Raising secure children matters. In fact, this chapter will talk about how it matters for your child's entire life. Becoming more secure yourself also matters, not only for your own happiness but also for the child you are raising. So, no matter what your financial status is, what your culture, your ethnicity, your educational level, no matter if you are two parents, one parent, or a divorced parent, a family-member parent, a stepparent, an adopted parent, a foster parent, or have any other configuration at home, the greatest gift you can give your child is a secure attachment. This book will show you what is known about secure children and the attachment they have with their parents.

SETTING THE SCENE: RECONNECTING WITH THE NATURAL INSTINCT FOR ATTACHMENT

The North Shore of Kauai is magical. It must certainly be a remnant of Eve's garden before chaos moved in. Silence, heavy with night, is only interrupted by breeze. In the morning, free-roaming roosters begin announcing the dawn before it appears. Birds rustle around calling out their locations. The air is balmy, and the temperature often matches the body's temperature, giving you the feeling of "wearing" the island. Moody weather rhythmically changes as trade winds bring periodic rain to bright sunny days. Egrets dress fields of tropical vegetation growing down to turquoise water, so dramatic in contrast that your eyes begin to drink in something ancient, something that feels lost but familiar ... the nonverbal rhythms of our bodies.

Looking out the kitchen window at the early morning Kauai rain, I contemplate who you are as the reader, where you are sitting in your life, and how we can together talk about matters of attachment for you and your child. It is my desire to help you find the world of the body, the world of feeling and instinct that so many of us have lost contact with. I do not consider "instinct" a fluffy idea to be put aside in favor of more verbal, abstract abilities but, instead, see our instincts as the bearers of feeling communications that are deep within the body. Instincts are ancient, shaped by evolution, and their expression needs to be understood, respected, and integrated into our thinking. You will learn in chapter 2 that the right cerebral hemisphere appears to house much of this nonverbal world of feeling and instinct. Too often, instincts and feelings have been corrupted by difficult or confusing childhoods that have led many of us into dark, lonely alleys as we try to find our way. Recovering the instinctual feeling world not only adds color and rhythm but also restores the fullness of feeling and meaning to our lives. With babies and young children, we must use our feelings and instincts to communicate. Carried by the forces of evolution, babies emerge from this deep biology into the waiting arms of their parents, who have different experiences, values, cultures, languages, and concepts held in their minds.

Sensitive and responsive caregiving given specifically in the early years of life fuels a child's development, and it produces secure children.

Within the security of these early relationships, babies grow with confidence and ultimately express their own interests and creativity using the stunning qualities of the conceptual, thinking mind. The body world has profound wisdoms of its own that are often lost to us as we live our busy lives. Babies, however, require us to release some of our urgent worldly matters and slide back into the rhythms of the body which nature has taken millions of years to create, a world where a child's connection to her parent matters for survival. We could not live without children, and not for the obvious reason that we need them to survive as a species. More importantly, children give us the delight of their innocence, the thrill of their discoveries, and the joy of their existence. They remind us of the beauty of naturalness. Without such reminders, our hearts would shrivel and die long before the human race.

Who you are, as the parent, matters too. Your values, your own early life experiences, your decisions about your children, all matter as they create the parameters of your unique family system in relation to your cultural surroundings. You may be now or will soon be a biological parent, you may be an adoptive or foster parent, or a relative or friend who is parenting or supporting parents. The fact is that attachment needs to matter to all of us, for secure attachment will directly improve the world we live in. This book will explore the inner workings of attachment, its role in the regulation of emotional states, and what it means for your child's overall development.

ATTACHMENT DEFINED

So what is *attachment?* In brief, attachment is a child's biological tie or bond to her primary caregivers, usually her parents. It is a biological system developed through evolution to protect the child, thus ensuring the likelihood she will grow into an adult and reproduce, thereby guaranteeing gene survival. The child's attachment to her parent is thought to develop over the first year of life. The degree of a child's attachment to her parent is shaped by the quality of sensitivity, attunement, and responsivity of the parent. Terms like *attachment* or *attachment bond* or *attachment tie* refer to the child's connection to her parents. The term *bonding*, however, is commonly used to refer to the parent's connection to the child. This bond can begin in pregnancy and be quite strong at birth. (For some mothers, however, the bond may take a bit of time to develop, especially if there is postpartum depression involved, or the baby was conceived in circumstances that were difficult for the mother; other causes for bonding difficulties will be discussed in chapter 3.) To be clear, *attachment* refers to the child's tie to the parent. To fully understand the significance of attachment, however, you will need to know about the history of attachment theory. By the end of this chapter, you will have a better appreciation for the importance of your child's forming attachment to you.

THE HISTORY OF ATTACHMENT THEORY

As reported by Robert Karen (1998), in the beginning of his career, British psychoanalyst John Bowlby put aside his medical training for a year to volunteer his services at a school for maladjusted children. The school itself was different from others in that, instead of using fear to control children's behavior, as was common at the time, it trained staff to be sensitive and available to the children while encouraging them to explore. Bowlby was quite taken by this approach and became especially interested in the early parent-child histories of the children whose behavior was so disturbed. He began to ask important questions about the impact of early parent-child experiences on children's behavior and, in particular, how children were attached to their caregivers, especially their mother.

Early Attachment Research

During the late 1940s and early 1950s, Bowlby's colleague James Robertson made a number of films showing the extreme distress of young children hospitalized without their parents. These heart-wrenching films showed a pattern to the child's response:

I. Protest: The child loudly called for the parent and could not be soothed by the staff.

2. Despair: The child collapsed emotionally when the parent did not return.

3. Detachment: The child detached, no longer cried for the parent, and acted *as if* she were no longer concerned.

Parents returning to pick up their child were shocked to find that their child was so different and made statements like "what happened to my child?" or "he was never the same after the hospital," or "I felt like she was adrift and didn't know who I was."

At that time in Britain as well as in the United States, parents were not allowed to stay in the hospital with their young child as it was mistakenly thought to be too disruptive for the child's healing. In fact, this idea continued well into the 1970s in the United States and was eventually changed primarily in response to Bowlby's work. For some children whose hospitalizations were reasonably short, parents later reported a clingy period and a preoccupation with the parent's whereabouts, but eventually these children were able to return to their former selves. For others who had longer hospitalizations, parents often reported that the child was never the same. These hospital disturbances led to a highly influential document written by Bowlby for the World Health Organization. In that document, he reviewed the severe deprivation found in children under five years old who had been put into foster or institutional homes where caretakers focused mainly on the physical care of the child but paid little attention to the child's emotional development (Bowlby 1952).

Bowlby (1988) had been influenced by Charles Darwin's work on natural selection, which continues to be the foundation for modern evolutionary theory. He was also impressed with Konrad Lorenz's work on ducklings. Lorenz noticed that a mother duck does not feed her ducklings directly but instead feeds them by showing the ducklings how to scratch and peck. Lorenz discovered that ducklings are genetically programmed to attach to the first moving object seen after hatching. Lorenz called this *imprinting*. Harry Harlow also demonstrated that an infant monkey removed from its mother at birth and "raised" by two wire mother monkeys showed a clear preference for the wire monkey that was dressed in cloth, rather than the wire monkey that fed it from a bottle (Bowlby 1988). It was thought that the infant monkey associated the cloth monkey with the natural holding and touching of a mother.

With these influences, Bowlby began to conceptualize a human biological attachment system refined by the forces of evolution. Specifically,
when stressed, afraid, or tired, a human baby will seek her primary caregiver and stay in close proximity to the caregiver until soothed. Bowlby
noted that children develop an attachment to the caregiver who takes
care of them during the first year, even if the caregiving is poor. While
there are certain cases where a child might not attach to her caregiver,
such as in some institutional settings, most children do develop an attachment to their caregivers. According to Bowlby, the attachment system is
not based upon feeding but instead upon protecting the child to ensure
the survival of the gene pool (Bowlby 1969/1982). This was a radical idea
at the time, as it was thought that children become attached to their
parents because they feed them. The new theory stated that a child's
behaviors, including crying, as well as following, clinging to, calling for,
and smiling at her parents, are instinctive attachment behaviors used
to keep the parent in close proximity to protect the child. It took Mary
Ainsworth, however, to clarify how a child attaches to her parent for
protection.

The Strange Situation Research Paradigm

Mary Ainsworth was a Canadian psychologist also trained in clinical
research. As told by Karen (1998), Ainsworth responded to an employment ad in the *London Times* looking for someone who could help organize data; John Bowlby had placed the ad. As a result of the Bowlby/
Ainsworth collaboration, it's now possible to measure the quality of a
child's attachment to her parent.

When Ainsworth's husband took a post in Uganda in the early
1950s, Ainsworth decided to study mother-infant pairs in their homes;
she proceeded to work with the tribal chiefs to do so. Over a nine-
month period, using an interpreter, she observed twenty-eight mother-
infant pairs for two hours every other week, tracking in great detail each
infant's development. Ainsworth not only confirmed Bowlby's impression that attachment does not have to do with feeding; she noted that
smiling, vocalization, and proximity to the mother were distinct enough
between infants that she could spot the mother based upon the child's
behavior alone (Karen 1998). Ainsworth noticed that as the children

began to take short excursions away from their mothers to explore their world, they were always aware of their mother's whereabouts. These children would also periodically return to the mother or smile at the mother while exploring. She conceptualized this movement as a child's use of the mother as a *secure base* from which to explore (Ainsworth 1967).

Two years later, in Baltimore, she repeated her observations in a study of twenty-six infants. Only this time she gathered expectant parents for her study and, with her research assistants, made home visits to chronicle the infants' development over the first year of life. She basically observed the same infant attachment behaviors in the Baltimore group that she had seen in Uganda, but it was harder to see the Baltimore infants using the mother as a secure base. She wondered if this was due to cultural differences, as the Baltimore infants were accustomed to seeing their mothers come and go, whereas the Ugandan infants were almost always in the presence of their mothers. This observation gave Ainsworth the idea of bringing the infants and mothers into the lab so that she could observe their attachment behaviors under mildly stressful conditions.

Ainsworth's investigations resulted in what is now known as the Strange Situation paradigm, which is to this day considered the gold standard for measuring a child's attachment to her parent when a child is between the ages of twelve and eighteen months. Strange Situation studies focus on gradually increasing an infant's stress to activate the biological attachment system so that it can be seen and measured. Again, when a young child is stressed, she will naturally seek her caregiver for protection, soothing, and reassurance. As she experiences mild to moderate stress, her behavior will reflect her expectations of what she has already learned from her caregiver about the caregiver's availability. It is by examining any difference in expectations that Strange Situation studies can determine the quality of a child's attachment to her caregiver.

A Note on Primary Attachment Relationships

Since much of Ainsworth's research was conducted on mothers and infants (although there are now a number of good father-infant Strange Situation studies), a word needs to be said about primary attachment relationships in general. The primary attachment figure for an infant is the person that the baby preferentially seeks out when stressed, tired, sick, afraid, or in need of soothing. In other words, a tired, fussy infant in a room with other adults will often continue to fuss until she is in the arms of her primary caregiver. In infancy (birth to eighteen months), the primary caregiver is usually the mother, with fathers beginning to be naturally approached by toddlers (nineteen to thirty-five months) and usually sought after by the preschooler (three to five years). In two-parent homes where the father is actively involved in the care of the baby (feeding, diapering, soothing, playing, and talking with), the baby may also consider the father a primary caregiver. However, even under these circumstances, when stressed, babies may still seek out their mothers. To reflect the composition of most of the studies, I will continue to refer to "mother" unless the study under discussion specifically examined other attachment figures, such as fathers or other caregivers. With that said, here's a look at the Strange Situation paradigm developed by Ainsworth.

The Strange Situation

The Strange Situation consists of eight three-minute episodes that are videotaped so that the researcher can later code the child's behavior.

1. The first episode consists of the mother and infant entering a room and finding toys in the middle of the room.

2. There are two chairs and the mother has been directed to sit in one of them while the infant explores the toys; this is episode 2.

3. While the infant is exploring the toys, a stranger enters (episode 3), is silent for a minute, and then begins talking with the mother.

4. Episode 4 begins when the mother leaves the room, and now the infant is left with the stranger.

5. In episode 5, the mother returns and the stranger leaves; this is the first mother-child reunion.

6. In episode 6, the mother leaves again, but this time the infant is alone.

7. Instead of the mother returning in episode 7, the stranger returns and tries to interact with the infant.

8. Mother now returns in episode 8, and the stranger leaves. Episode 8 is the second mother-child reunion. Researchers observe how the baby reacts to the mother at both reunions, and this information is used to determine the child's attachment category (Ainsworth et al. 1978).

attachment syste
c way c interacts w
primary when u ha
in need of caregiver

ORGANIZED ATTACHMENT STYLES

Ainsworth found three organized attachment styles, or categories: *secure*, *insecure-avoidant*, and *insecure-ambivalent*. The term *attachment style* is defined as the child's way of behaving with her primary attachment figure when she is in need of the caregiver, that is, when her inborn attachment system has been activated. A child's attachment style reflects the history of parent-child interaction and her parent's ongoing response to her biological attachment needs. You also may have heard the terms *attachment categories* and *attachment strategies*, both of which are commonly used in research. In general, all three terms refer to a child's way of behaving when the attachment system is activated. Secure, insecure-avoidant, and insecure-ambivalent styles are all *organized* attachment styles, meaning that the child's approach to the parent is predictable and consistent in style. Main and Solomon (1990) found a fourth category called *disorganized/disoriented attachment*. This category is not a style but, rather, a phenomenon that is highly associated with abuse. I will discuss it in greater depth later in the chapter.

The Secure Attachment Style

Infants coded *secure* are quite upset when their mother leaves and seek close proximity to her when she returns. Secure infants maintain

15

close contact with their mother until they feel soothed enough to explore again. What is noteworthy is that secure infants are very easily soothed by their mothers and return to exploring the toys within a short time. Secure infants are thought to soothe easily because the child knows the mother will respond sensitively to her, for this is what the child has experienced already. In other words, the child has no doubt that her mother will respond to her needs. Growing up is about exploring for a mastery of tasks required at each developmental stage, and a child must rely on the sensitivity of her parent to help her feel secure enough to explore.

The Insecure-Avoidant Attachment Style

Infants coded *insecure-avoidant* have a style of not approaching their mother for reassurance, even when they want it. Instead, the insecure-avoidant infant may not leave the toys when her mother is gone (although the child's play is diminished and dampened). The infant may not even look at her mother or may even actively turn away from her mother when she returns. Although the avoidant child looks calm (and one might be inclined to say this child has a level of mastery the secure child doesn't have, for she is able to take care of herself while her mother is gone), a growing amount of research measuring stress hormones and monitoring heart rates shows that avoidant children are in fact very distressed when separated from their mothers (Spangler and Grossmann 1993; Zelenko et al. 2005).

Again, it is thought that the avoidant child is reflecting her experience with her mother, who has provided limited care of her needs, who is often rejecting of the child's need to attach, in particular, and who tends to push the child toward premature independence. This child already knows that her mother will not respond well to her needs for reassurance, so she doesn't even approach. There are multiple studies showing that mothers of insecure-avoidant children can be harsh, rejecting, and lack tenderness (Lyons-Ruth 1996).

The Insecure-Ambivalent Attachment Style

Infants coded *insecure-ambivalent* seek the mother at reunion. However, these infants may show anger at their mother, may kick or hit their mother, and can increase their distress to the point of throwing a tantrum. What is noteworthy is that infants coded ambivalent are not soothed by their mother's attention, and they do not return to exploring the toys. Often the mother will try to put the child down (as she has been instructed to do by the researcher), but the child will cling to her mother, continually fuss, show signs of anger, perhaps arch her back and kick, and often refuse to be put down.

It is thought that the ambivalent child's experience with her mother has been inconsistent, so the child has developed a strategy that exaggerates her needs to keep her mother close by and oriented to her. In contrast to the avoidant child who knows how her mother will respond, the ambivalent child doesn't know if her mother will respond "this time" to her needs for reassurance. The ambivalent strategy, therefore, is geared to orient the mother as often as possible because the child never knows when the mother will be available. Studies show that mothers of insecure-ambivalent children actually are promoting dependency in their children that interferes with the autonomy needed for development (Cassidy and Berlin 1994).

By correlating data from the Strange Situation with data taken in the home, Ainsworth found that secure infants had more sensitive mothers. The correlation between mother sensitivity to her infant's signals and infant security has been found in an analysis of multiple published studies (the scientific term for this is *meta-analysis*) of mother-infant pairs (De Wolff and van IJzendoorn 1997). Parent sensitivity associated with infant security has also been found for fathers (van IJzendoorn and De Wolff 1997). Ainsworth also found that infants in both of the insecure categories (avoidant and ambivalent) cried more at home and were more angry and noncompliant than were infants who were coded secure. Mothers of insecure infants were not only generally less sensitive and less accessible to their infants; they were also more interfering (Ainsworth et al. 1978). Here's a look at Kyle and his family, as an example of a secure attachment in action.

Fun at the Beach: Kyle and the Boogie Board

On the south shore of Kauai, Poipu Beach is known for its reasonable waves and kiddie cove that families with young children can enjoy. There is also a lifeguard station, so parents feel some freedom from water worries. Kyle was a handsome eighteen- to twenty-month-old child with long hair at the beach with his family. Kyle had a seventeen-inch mini-boogie board replete with a leash that was strapped to his leg. Kyle and his father were heading down to the water's edge to play while his mother sat in the sand close by. Kyle put one toe in the water, screamed (a scream that said, *I'm not going in there!* and *I better make this known to Mom!*), and headed for his mother. He backed up into her, and she soothed him, talked with him, and then changed the leash to the other ankle (brilliant mom) and sent him on his way. Kyle returned to his dad, who encouraged him to return to the water. Kyle put a toe in, screamed, and returned to his mom, cuddled in briefly, then stood to one side of her. His mom changed the boogie board leash to his arm and sent him back again. Kyle returned to the water, screeched (a screech that now said *this might be okay*), and returned to his mother; only this time he stood in front of her, at a distance, removed the leash himself, and tried new spots like his head (it seemed that the leash didn't work there), his waist (same problem), and so on. Kyle's dad now came over and walked him to the water, letting Kyle hold the boogie board in front of him. His dad led him to the water, and before Kyle realized what had happened, his father had him on the board, and he caught a mini wave. Kyle did a visual check-in with his mother, not his father. This check-in is called *visual referencing*, as the young toddler moved from the need to be physically reassured by his mother to using only a visual reading of his mother about the appropriateness of this riding-the-waves game. Kyle now got out of the water, went to his mother, received a "good job!" from her, and then with no prodding, returned to his dad and the water. Kyle took another small wave with his dad's help, and then returned to his mom for breastfeeding.

Contrast this story with how the same parents interacted with their four-year-old son, Aidan, in the water. His father was standing in the water when an unexpected wave caught Aidan, and he got thoroughly dunked. Aidan immediately looked at his dad who was laughing, indicating, "That was fun!" Aidan then got out of the water, stood at the water's edge, and hollered at his mom, "Did you see that? I almost drowned!" The water was only about a half-foot deep, Aidan's father was about a foot away, and Aidan was laughing. Aidan's mom gave a high sign and smiled. Aidan looked at his dad proudly and wanted to do it again.

Here we see the shift in parental referencing to the father with only a very brief mother reference. The preschooler has a strong willingness and interest in playing with his father. During both of these interactions with their children, both of the parents visually referenced each other. Mom and Dad are not only able to read their children's nonverbal cues; they are also able to use and understand their own nonverbal communication with each other.

Now take a moment to look more closely at some of the issues I have been discussing. Can you see Kyle's attachment? Who is the primary attachment figure for Kyle? Do you see the difference for Aidan? What attachment behaviors has Kyle shown? What about Aidan? Do you see that attachment is serving a regulatory function? Is Kyle and Aidan's mother sensitive or insensitive? How about their father? Do you see Kyle's movement between exploration and proximity-seeking with his mother? Do you see how this changes for Aidan? How does Kyle's mother react to Kyle when he approaches her? Do you see how the father interacts one way with Kyle and another way with Aidan? Can you describe the difference?

You can see from this family interaction that Kyle mastered his first ride on the boogie board because his mother was able to read his hesitancy (some fear) yet provided a frame (try the leash on the other leg and see if that works) to support mastery. The famous Russian psychologist Lev Vygotsky pointed out that a child's actual ability to solve problems has to be seen in relationship to what her potential is when she's problem solving under the guidance of an adult (Vygotsky 1978). This process has been referred to as the parent scaffolding the task. In other words, the parent provides mini-steps for the child to master the task.

Just as a jasmine plant needs a lattice to grow on, children require these parent- and teacher-provided footholds to keep their emotions within a range that allows them to learn skills and master tasks. Anyone who has spoken in public or taken a test knows the importance of keeping your anxiety in check, as too much anxiety can prevent you from performing well. Kyle's mother actively helps Kyle lower the anxiety (or fear or stress) that is building up in his unseen nervous system, as she provides ongoing reassurance and mini-step solutions to a problem. She is balancing his fear and stress through soothing, encouragement, and active participation in solving the problem. Kyle's mother was so successful that eventually Kyle took his mother's lead and made some suggestions of his own! This developmental support is called *emotional regulation*; that is, Kyle's mother is intimately involved in helping her child maintain his emotions within a range that allows for balance and exploration. In fact, she is *co-regulating* her child's emotional state; the mother is using her own emotional state as the model for which the child can match or synchronize his emotions. This is the road to security, and this is the road that leads to emotional self-regulation.

Kyle's father also supported Kyle's mastery by coordinating and referencing his interactions based upon cues from Kyle's mother. This is a wonderful example of mother, father, and family attunement, which you will soon see is one of the most important qualities (if not the most) for raising secure children. If you are by chance a member of this family who was in Kauai in July 2006, go forth and teach others!

What Kyle Learned

Here are two questions that I will ask periodically throughout this book: "What has the child learned?" and "Whose needs are being met?" As a practicing clinical psychologist working with adults, children, and families, as well as training master- and doctoral-level interns in early parent-child relationships from birth to age five, I find these to be the two most important questions to ask when evaluating how well we are reading a child's internal, nonverbal world of feeling. I also teach parents to ask these questions as tools to remind themselves that young children are learning more from what you do and how you look and sound (that is, what your right hemisphere is communicating) than from what you say. When you are in the throes of parenting, it is all too easy to assume a verbal left-brain parenting stance and forget that your child is responding more to your nonverbal communications.

What has Kyle learned from his mother? He has learned that she understands that this wave riding is a very big, somewhat scary deal.

At his age, this thought wouldn't be conscious, but it would be felt. He also learned that his mother is okay with wave riding, so it must not be that bad, and she actively helped him master it by suggesting that perhaps trying another way (leash on another limb) would help. Kyle was reading and experiencing his mother's face and body reactions, which were all saying, "Nothing horrible is happening." Now suppose his mother had heard his scream, left her towel quickly with fear on her face, run up to him, grabbed him in her arms, and kissed him, saying, "We won't do this today." What would he have learned? He would have learned that there is something dangerous about this wave riding stuff, just as he suspects! His mother's reactivity alone would confirm to him, "Yep, this is dangerous alright!" But Kyle's mother didn't do this. Instead she calmly provided mini-steps (scaffolding) for him to be successful with wave riding.

What has Kyle learned from his father? He has learned that his father can tolerate his need for mother check-ins without getting flustered or angry or worried. He also learned that his dad could make this boogie-board-riding-wave-thing happen! Dad made the physical task of wave riding happen with ease, and Mom provided with ease what was needed to manage his internal feelings, which in this instance were more on the fear spectrum, as she soothed him and scaffolded the task. The result is that Kyle's success likely felt seamless to him and quite matter-of-fact. Now what has Kyle learned about his parents? He has learned through experience (feeling) that they both support his mastery for wave riding by working in tandem. He also had this wonderful experience of feeling the differences in how his mother and father encourage him.

Lastly, whose needs were being met? In this situation, clearly it was the needs of the child. *Attunement*, then, is the ability to understand and respond to a child's inner-feeling world while encouraging mastery of the external world. As you can see, Kyle's parents were doing this. You might also say that, as parents, they felt a need to help their child succeed in skills and independence, but clearly they were focused on supporting the primary need of the child. You can easily see Kyle's attachment to his mother and father. You can see that the attachment to his mother is primary. Even though his father may be a primary attachment figure, he is more secondary for Kyle at this age than he is for four-year-old Aidan.

DISORGANIZED ATTACHMENT

As mentioned earlier, Ainsworth's student Mary Main and a colleague discovered a fourth category that was not an organized strategy to cope with the temporary loss of the mother. They called this fourth strategy *disorganized/disoriented* (Main and Solomon 1990), and it differs greatly from the other three categories. While coding Strange Situation episodes, Mary Main noticed that some infants appeared to become disorganized in the presence of their mother, and their behavior on approach was also very different from that of the insecure children. She found that disorganized approaches often included distraction, dissociation, and signs of fear and confusion, giving the coder the impression that the attachment system had broken down completely. For example, infants coded disorganized may start to approach their mother, then veer off toward the wall or, upon seeing her, hide behind a chair, or follow the stranger out of the room, or begin to hit their head or twirl in circles or use other distracting behaviors.

Disorganization is generally the result of trauma, and it is associated with more serious mental health problems (Carlson 1998; Lyons-Ruth 1996; van IJzendoorn, Schuengel, and Bakermans-Kranenburg 1999). With disorganized children, there is a breakdown in the attachment strategy altogether, as the parent is both feared and sought after at the same time. Parents of disorganized children need help themselves, for there are generally multiple issues involved; in many cases, parents of disorganized children suffered abuse or neglect as children.

Chaos in a Grocery Store: Childhood Disorganization

It is easy to understand disorganization when the trauma is observable. Let's look at an example. A friend of mine was in the produce aisle at the grocery store when she heard three-year-old Johnny crying. His mother was screaming at him and then began "pummeling" his head with her hand. Shocked, my friend started over toward the mother when she saw his mother push Johnny away and leave the aisle. Johnny, now screaming "Mommy, Mommy," ran after her. Appalled by this, my friend explained, "He had nowhere else to go, so he ran to her and pulled on her. As if to do him a favor, she picked him up."

In every state in the country, child protective services could have taken Johnny from his mother if this incident were reported. My friend reported the incident to the manager of the store, but she did not know the final outcome. Although it would be the physical beating of the child that triggered the report, the true horror is what goes unseen. For the child, the person he loves the most is breaking his heart and threatening to throw him away. It is easy for us to see the fault of the mother, but what is harder to see is that the mother was likely treated in a similar fashion by her parents. As you know, the story could have just as easily been about an abusing father. In all cases, the parent and child are in trouble and need help.

My friend was struck with how Johnny was desperately running after his mother even though she was so cruel to him. Disorganization in a child shows us the power of attachment, because when a young child is afraid, she will still seek the primary attachment figure, even if the attachment figure is the abuser. In this case, the child also felt the stress of being abandoned in a big store with strangers.

COMPARING ORGANIZED AND DISORGANIZED ATTACHMENT

One way to think about attachment is that nature has provided internal biological tracks for securing a child's protection. The pattern of the tracks, however, is dependent upon the quality of parenting, particularly a parent's ability to tune in or attune to a child's internal state and budding mind. With secure children, parents respond with sensitivity to the child's needs, allowing the child to move naturally into exploration of the world. This child has a secure and organized attachment system, because when the child's attachment system is activated, the parent is able to deactivate it, thus allowing the child to move on. For avoidant children, the child has learned to avoid the parent in response to parental harshness, humiliation, and/or rejection. The avoidant child also has an organized attachment system in that it is predictable to the child, but the cost is chronic insecurity and a lack of emotional skills. Parents of avoidant children encourage them not to approach, focusing more on independence, thereby chronically deactivating the child's attachment system. For ambivalent children, the child has learned to stay very close to the parent, in case the parent might respond this time. This child also has an organized attachment system, in that the strategy is predictable and will get the child a response from the parent some of the time, but again the cost is a lack of security. Parents of ambivalent children keep the child's attachment system chronically hyperactivated.

Disorganization, on the other hand, does not present itself in any consistent way, and there is no one pattern. Rather, disorganized behaviors are quite unique to a particular child's characteristics and experience. Children showing signs of disorganization in the Strange Situation are also given an organized attachment category, as disorganized behaviors may only appear when the child is under stress. When stress is within reasonable ranges, the child's attachment strategy may appear more organized. Disorganization in the attachment system is a serious condition that, if chronic, can severely affect brain organization; it is highly associated with child abuse. In fact, in one study of maltreated children, 82 percent were disorganized (Carlson et al. 1989).

In studies following children coded in the Strange Situation into adulthood (Sroufe et al. 2005), disorganized attachment has been associated with serious adult psychopathology. Perhaps more disquieting, the next generation (children of these children) showed signs of disorganization. In a seminal paper called "Ghosts in the Nursery," which was based upon in-home work with parents and infants, Selma Fraiberg and colleagues found that infant-parent problems were sometimes caused by unresolved conflicts that the parent had with her own parents, and these conflicts could be projected onto the baby (Fraiberg, Adelson, and Shapiro 1975). In attachment theory, what was triggered and projected onto the child in the grocery store was the mother's own internal working model based upon her own attachment history.

There are many parents, however, who have come from difficult backgrounds and are raising their children differently from how they were raised. These parents may be more resilient by nature, have supportive partners and families, or are exerting sheer will to not raise their children the way they were brought up. I will talk more about support systems and their importance for adult emotional regulation in chapter 3.

In case you are feeling overwhelmed by all this new information, I want to note here that you don't have to be perfect to be a good parent. At the end of this chapter, I will talk about the importance of being good enough, not perfect. I will also talk further about how you don't have to parent the way you were parented. If you are at all concerned about your own parenting skills, feel free to skip to the end of this chapter before continuing on.

INTERNAL WORKING MODELS: WE ALL HAVE EARLY CHILDHOOD EXPERIENCES

The internal working model was a term that Bowlby (1969/1982) and Ainsworth (Ainsworth et al. 1978) used to describe the internally encoded attachment experience a child has with her primary attachment figures. These experiences are encoded directly into the circuitry of the brain and can be triggered by events in the present moment. As I have discussed, there are strategy differences in the internal working models of secure, insecure-avoidant, and insecure-ambivalent children. As noted too, the experience encoded for children categorized as disorganized is noteworthy for a lack of strategy. Because our own attachment histories influence our parenting styles, they matter not only for the quality of our own lives but also for the quality of the lives of our children as they enter the world with us as their primary guides.

The pattern by which you respond to your child's attachment needs will influence your child's overall development, particularly the quality of her social and emotional development. For the secure child, development runs relatively smoothly because her parents are reading her cues, and when things are off track, they are actively trying to get her back on track. For insecure children, however, the home environment has altered the biological attachment tracks in significant enough ways to make development more challenging. For disorganized children, the ruts are dug deeply enough to disastrously derail development.

ATTACHMENT CATEGORIES OVER TIME

Alan Sroufe and his colleagues in the Minnesota Parent-Child Project have been following high-risk mother-infant pairs coded in the Strange Situation for twenty-six years (Sroufe et al. 2005). In fact, the infants studied are now adults having their own children. This research laboratory has produced extraordinary data on the nature of attachment categories over time. Overall, the researchers have found differences in socioemotional, behavioral, and problem-solving abilities, with secure children showing more emotional regulation than insecure children. There are now multiple studies from other laboratories suggesting that secure children score cognitively higher on standard tests than do insecure children; this may be due to the flexibility in attentional resources (Main 2000) found in emotionally regulated children. In the Minnesota study, when the children were twelve to eighteen months old, the children coded secure were more cooperative with teachers and other children and more interested in mastery of games in middle childhood (Sroufe et al. 2005). Secure children who grow into secure adults seem to also find mates who are secure. Adults in secure-secure relationships seem to provide more support to each other, have less conflict in their relationships, and are more responsive to their children (Belsky 1999). Here is a look at what secure children learn, followed by a look at what insecure children learn.

WHAT SECURE CHILDREN LEARN

Children whose parents respond to them with greater sensitivity learn the following:

- They can get their needs met, so they have a greater ability to explore the world.

- They can explore their world with confidence and autonomy, for they know their parents are available when needed.

- They can influence others and be successful in the world, for they have been successful in getting their needs met by their parents and their parents have provided the footholds (scaffolding) needed for task mastery.

- They can engage in reciprocal interactions with others, for they have learned reciprocity from their parents.

- They can meet their own needs, for their parents met theirs.

- They can be empathetic toward others, for they have learned from their parents that when one is in need, the other responds.

- They are socially competent, for they have learned from their parents that responsive, respectful interactions are possible.

- They are worthy of positive and trusting social interactions, for they have had positive and trusting interactions with their parents.

- They can regulate their emotions themselves, for their parents were able to show them how.

- They can have future successful relationships, for they have had a successful relationship with their parents.

- Based upon all the above, they learn that they are competent, lovable, cooperative, and capable.

In the Minnesota study (Sroufe et al. 2005), children coded secure in preschool were less dependent upon teachers and had more peer interaction than did the insecure children. In middle school summer camps, secure children continued to have less contact with adults and more contact with peers, and this continued into the high school years. Secure children were more persistent, enthusiastic, and more flexible about learning tasks, and they increased their effort (unlike insecure children) when they believed they were failing on a task. They were able to handle frustration more easily. Secure children were neither bullies nor the victims of bullies, and they displayed less anxiety and anger toward others. Teacher ratings found secure children more socially competent beginning in preschool. By middle childhood, secure children formed more peer relationships with other secure children and were more respectful of social interaction rules than were insecure children. By adolescence, secure teens continued to be more respectful and confident in mixed-gender functions, and they continued to be rated by teachers as more competent. Although attachment cannot explain all of development, it does appear to provide the social-emotional foundation needed to produce secure, cooperative, and competent children.

WHAT INSECURE-AVOIDANT AND -AMBIVALENT CHILDREN LEARN

Children whose parents do not respond to them with sensitivity but instead either reject them and their need for physical contact and/or are inconsistent in their parenting responses learn the following:

- They cannot get their needs met because their parents did not meet them; therefore they develop defensive strategies that compromise exploration.

- They are not confident and autonomous, since being alone to explore without a responsive caregiver triggers fears that their care and protection will be unavailable or inconsistent should they feel afraid.

- They believe their efforts will be unsuccessful, for their efforts to influence their parents have failed.

- They can't regulate their emotions, for their parents have not consistently been available to help them regulate their emotions.

- They do not expect to be successful in getting their needs met, for they weren't successful with their parents.

In the Minnesota study (Sroufe et al. 2005), children coded avoidant in infancy were less cooperative in middle childhood. In fact, many of these children were aggressive and were considered bullies. As would be expected, they appeared to not know how to interact cooperatively with other children. In preschool, avoidant children were often bullies and their victims more often the ambivalent children. Avoidant children also engaged more in blaming others for their actions and were more hostile than the other children. Since middle childhood is a time when children form peer or buddy relationships, these children's relationship disadvantages began to stand out, and often they were isolated because other children refused to play with them. Avoidant children seem to develop a more hostile-aggressive strategy. Perhaps to cope with the rejection they experience with their caregivers, they become the aggressors themselves. This strategy has been associated with conduct disorders as well as depression. Avoidant children often grow up and select other insecure mates. These relationships have been found to have more conflict and less support than secure-secure partnerships (Belsky 1999).

Ambivalent children were judged to be the most dependent, often not wanting to leave the teacher's side and generally were found to be more anxious, less assertive, and more hesitant about new experiences than secure or avoidant children. Children coded ambivalent were found to be clinging to teachers, were often afraid, and were often the victims of the bullies. Ambivalent children seem to develop a constant vigilance about getting their needs met, a strategy that increases their likelihood of receiving whatever care might be offered. This strategy, however, has been associated with anxiety disorders as well as depression. Ambivalent children often grow up to be caretakers and also tend to select insecure mates who have less sensitivity (Belsky 1999). It has been my experience that women receiving inconsistent caregiving in their childhoods are often overly preoccupied with caregiving even at the expense of their autonomy.

In general, insecure children have been found to be more dependent than secure children and less flexible when frustrated. In the Minnesota study (Sroufe et al. 2005), insecure toddlers were less persistent on tasks. In preschool, insecure children sought teacher attention more often than did secure children and at the expense of developing peer interactions. In a related study, insecure preschoolers actually decreased their effort when they thought they were failing, unlike the secure children, who increased their effort under the same conditions (Lutkenhaus, Grossmann, and Grossmann, 1985). In adolescence, the insecure children continued to be more dependent on adults than secure children. Insecure children have been found to have more negative emotions, such as anger and aggression, than secure children. Insecure children were more likely to be angry and aggressive toward their mother during a task than were secure children. In video ratings of children in distress and the responses of children in the vicinity, the avoidant children were less empathetic than the secure children, and the ambivalent children, although empathetic, seemed to "have trouble maintaining a boundary between someone else's distress and their own" (Weinfield et al. 1999, 79).

WHAT DISORGANIZED CHILDREN LEARN

Disorganized children are in harm's way and are generally terrified by their parent(s). The disorganized classification has been associated with serious adult psychopathology in the parent, including alcoholism, drug use, chronic depressive states, and physical, sexual, and emotional abuse and neglect—in short, maltreating parents. Disorganization has also been found in violent offenders (Karr-Morse and Wiley 1997). Children whose parents are frightening, violent, and/or grossly neglectful cannot easily learn or freely explore because so much of their attention is focused on survival. Instead, what disorganized children seem to struggle with is how to survive. Some of the fallout of living in survival mode is that it teaches the child more how to do the following:

- They develop any strategy that reduces terror, including distraction, dissociation, and/or aggression or withdrawal, for their parents are frightening to them.

- They avoid intimacy in relationships, for they have experienced danger and confusion in their first relationships.

- They become vigilant and distrustful, for they have experienced harm, gross inconsistency, and/or extreme neglect from their parents.

- They passively accept what others give, as they have learned they have no power to affect their world, for they couldn't affect their parents.

- They get what is needed in any way possible, for they have learned that their parents could not be loving and caring to them and that they have to fend for themselves.

Mary Main and Erik Hesse now postulate that frightening behavior in the parent is one of the leading hypotheses for understanding child-hood disorganization (Main and Hesse 1990). This is important for us to know, as the implication is that to disorganize a child, a parent doesn't have to fit the standard physical, sexual, emotional, and/or negligent abuse categories used by most child protective services in the United States. In fact, a parent who cannot read a child's escalating fear of the parent in a game of chase, even when the child is not laughing or is actively turning away, but instead continues to pursue the child with growling sounds that are terrifying to the child, can lead to disorganization, especially when the parent's behavior is chronic.

TEMPERAMENT AND ATTACHMENT

Before leaving this discussion of childhood attachment categories, I need to say a few words about temperament. Even though it is now believed that gene expression is mediated by environmental experience (Moore 2001), children are born uniquely themselves, often with different temperaments. No two children are alike, as most parents of twins will tell you. There has been an ongoing argument that it is the temperament of a child that determines the attachment category, not parent sensitivity. This has proven to be false in a number of studies (Carlson 1998; van IJzendoorn, Schuengel, and Bakermans-Kranenburg 1999), including a genetic study (Bokhorst et al. 2003).

Attachment research has repeatedly shown that secure parents seem to be able to accommodate challenging temperaments and raise secure children. For shy children, parents will engage in more scaffold-ing as they try to encourage their child to try. Bold children will require more direction and firmer boundaries; therefore, some temperaments do require more from parents than would an easy baby. The additional work that goes into raising a child with a challenging temperament, then, may be easier for secure parents. Insecure parents and parents that are unresolved with respect to their own trauma may be much more challenged by temperamental differences in their children.

YOU DON'T HAVE TO PARENT THE WAY YOU WERE PARENTED

Many of us will have primarily loving memories of our own childhood (interspersed with the normal complaints) with responsive parents who provided a coherent-enough family life for us. Some of us, though, will remember frustrating childhoods where parents were unpredictable and sometimes scary. Still others will have experienced a lack of parental interaction and interest in our lives. And sadly, some of us will have experienced the disorganization and confusion of parental abuse. Since what goes around seems to come around again, only this time in your children, at times you will need to ask yourself the hard questions about who you are as a parent, what your children learn from you, and whose needs are being met. It's important to consciously reflect on what you want and don't want to pass on to your children, for what you experienced in your own childhood can affect how you parent.

How parents talk about their early childhoods has been found to predict the attachment category of their unborn child. The Adult Attachment Interview (AAI; George, Kaplan, and Main 1984, 1985, 1996) was the result of this serendipitous finding that has given us a way to measure an adult's state of mind with respect to attachment. This powerful instrument produces four adult attachment categories that correspond with and predict the infant categories with about 75 percent accuracy (Hesse 1999; van IJzendoorn and Bakermans-Kranenburg 1996). The adult classifications are *secure/autonomous, dismissive, preoccupied,* and *unresolved/disorganized* states of mind that correspond to the baby classifications determined from the Strange Situation as secure, avoidant, ambivalent, and disorganized, respectively. Even when the AAI is given in pregnancy, it will predict the attachment category of a mother's yet unborn child when the child is a year old with 69 percent accuracy (van IJzendoorn 1995).

How is it possible that a parent's state of mind with respect to attachment can predict the attachment category of a yet unborn child? As you enter into the world of the brain and the powerful interaction between environment and neurobiology, you will be better able to see what might be the connection between parental states of mind, parental behavior, and a child's development and sense of security. The ability to self-reflect appears to be one of the more important elements associated with secure attachment in an adult (Fonagy et al. 1991). The tumultuous eruptions, stabilizations, and integrations of development during the first five years of life are stunning to experience as cognition, language, motor skill, social-emotional, and family systems evolve and intertwine in your developing child. These experiences are so awe-inspiring that they can change you. If you can reflect on your experiences and learn from them, however, you can make choices to do things differently.

PARENTS NEED TO BE GOOD ENOUGH, NOT PERFECT

If you are beginning to feel somewhat overwhelmed with what it takes to raise a secure child, the developmental psychoanalyst Donald Winnicott suggested a number of years ago that all that is needed is a "good enough" or "an ordinary mother" or parent (Winnicott 1965). Bowlby also referred to the ordinary mother. Through video, the infant researcher Ed Tronick has shown us the intensely interactive nature of infant-parent emotional states and reminds us that infant development is not smooth. Contrary to perhaps culturally idealized mother-child interactions, Tronick stresses that the empirical evidence shows that the ordinary mother has moderate levels of infant-state attunement with equal amounts of time spent in misattunement and repair (Tronick 2006). In psychology, what most do is considered the standard. So you can see that nature is quite forgiving, and children can be raised nicely without supermoms or -dads, as long as you can detect misattunements and engage in attunement repairs most of the time. In fact, you don't want perfect attunement. Perfect attunement decreases the range of what a baby can tolerate and interferes with the development of healthy coping responses. You don't want chronic misattunement either, as the baby can't develop emotional regulation. Moderate levels of attunement are actually considered more beneficial for development. Lastly, Main, Hesse, and Kaplan (2005) suggest that a number of people who have had difficult childhoods, including childhoods with abuse, code secure on the AAI. They call this category of security *earned secure*.

As a long-practicing clinical psychologist using attachment and affect regulation theories to treat adults, children, and families, I have come to see that many of us have had our own basic instincts corrupted by perhaps well-intended but misdirected guidance. Many women treated in psychotherapy have a history of not trusting themselves; many men come from pasts where expressing feelings was considered unmanly and actively repressed. In a strange way, children expose the hurts in us by merely arriving in innocence ready to love, play, and make meaning. They are unaware of the ongoing commitment, care, and responsibility it requires of the parent. Seeing your child smile at you, though, pushes some internal delete button for the stress of the day. You need to be able to respond to these signals from your child. One way to be more responsive to your child's cues is to have a support system in place—such as time to yourself, a supportive community of friends and family or a supportive spouse—that will help you refuel so that you can have more energy for your child. I will continually talk about your support system, as it can break children's hearts when you can't meet them in the body world, where the nonverbal reigns and instincts light the way.

IN A NUTSHELL: ATTACHMENT SECURITY IS BUILT WITH PARENTAL ATTUNEMENT AND SENSITIVITY

CHAPTER 2

What's Behind the Face

Perhaps the most important revelation in human split-brain research is precisely this: that the left cerebral hemisphere of humans is prone to fabricating verbal narratives that do not necessarily accord with the truth.
—Antonio R. Damasio, *The Feeling of What Happens*

Babies feel before they think. In fact, babies communicate with us through feeling states. When babies are hungry, there is a feeling; when wet, a feeling here too. Babies have contented feelings, gnawing feelings, aversive feelings, startled feelings, curious feelings, excited feelings, and many other feelings that they express outwardly through subtle facial changes, gazing, head turning, whole-body movements, and vocalizations. Being able to interpret your baby's feeling states is the key to understanding what your baby is communicating through his body. Responding with sensitivity to your baby's communications and needs is what attunement is all about.

As discussed in chapter 1, a baby's secure attachment to his parents emerges from an ongoing lived experience with sensitive and responsive parents who tune in to their baby's *body world* using their own nonverbal abilities, instincts, and feelings. The world of instinct and nonverbal-to-nonverbal communication is a primary force, one that underlies all of our actions and perhaps all of our thought as well. It appears to be nature's gift to all of us for our protection throughout life. When words are accurately enough coupled with what we communicate with our bodies, babies perceive us as a whole and develop authentically and securely into themselves with the ability to feel what is true. This incredibly important guidance system is ancient, instinctual, and nonverbal, and it appears to be the result of complex interactions in the brain.

Parents play critical roles in modulating their baby's arousal levels, which are associated with the baby's internal physiology and brain development. The key to being a sensitive parent is to be aware of your baby's level of arousal and to respond accordingly. Arousal naturally decreases in sleepy babies and increases in excited, playful babies. Babies who have been crying hard (for instance, when they have just gotten their shots and are feeling lousy) need their parents to soothe them and reduce their arousal. Parents may try to soothe their baby through holding, using soft words about how horrible it all was, and/or breast- or bottle-feeding. But soothing, or lowering arousal, is not the only help that babies need. Babies who chronically do not have enough interaction will appear listless, flat, and have very low levels of arousal, which can also be felt as aversive. These babies are in need of increased energy in order to feel alive and cared for.

This chapter will discuss how attunement affects your baby's internal guidance system and development. Again, through connection and attunement, you are actively regulating your baby's internal physiology and thereby creating balance in your baby's nervous system, and this balance is needed for attention, learning, and exploration. When you regulate your infant's nervous system, your infant will feel a positive state of balance. This is the beginning of your baby's feelings of confidence. When your baby directly experiences your ability to reduce his experience of negative or aversive feelings in his body, he begins to trust you, for he knows you can make his awful feelings better. This trust is the foundation for a secure attachment. It is also how *home* (and all that this means) is carried with us wherever we go. It is the foundation upon which our verbal language develops and rests. Is home healthy, safe, and secure or rejecting, inconsistent, or terrorizing? In order to thoroughly understand the connection between lived experience and brain development, you will need to know more about the world of neurons, synapses, and the critical brain connections needed in the early years of life.

SETTING THE SCENE: VISUALIZING THE INTERIOR WORLD OF THE BRAIN

For those of us who fly a lot, taking the train is a very different experience. First of all, they just go. No need to fasten your seat belt, no waiting for permission to take off, no powering up to lift off—nothing. They just start. It's eerie because you might have just found a seat and are settling in when you notice the landscape is moving past your window.

Trains can't go anywhere without tracks, of course. And tracks accumulate as you approach bustling stations. For example, when approaching Los Angeles Union Station from San Diego, the tracks increase in number from one or two to over ten. If you've ever been to Chicago Union Station or Penn Station in New York City, you would have found a field of tracks as you approached these stations. This is because trains from many locations are all converging to a point: the station. Through careful communication from dispatch (whatever and wherever this is), a train threads its way down the correct track, often crossing many others before it arrives at the desired station. Another interesting and sometimes challenging property of trains is that the route is not always direct, for the tracks have been laid in locations based upon common use.

Similarly, the neural tracks laid down in a baby's brain are based upon use. That is, the organization of these tracks is dependent upon and specific to the baby's early caregiving experiences. To see how your relationship affects your child's development, it's important to look at how his brain develops. To begin, you'll need to learn a little brain-speak, which I'll illustrate with examples.

ENTRAINMENT: SYNCHRONIZING TWO SYSTEMS

The word *entrainment* is a commonly used term in research (especially in research on biological rhythms); it indicates the synchronization or resonance of one system to another. *Entrainment* is the process by which two separate rhythms or systems begin to move into one synchronized movement because of close proximity to the other; that is, both rhythms begin to assume the same shape. *Synchrony, resonance*, and *attunement* all describe the process of parents being close enough to direct, modulate, and synchronize their own biological rhythms, feelings, and communications to the emerging rhythms, feeling states, and communications of their infant. In fact, *synchrony* and *resonance* are other ways to describe the processes involved in attunement. Parents who synchronize their own feeling states to the feeling states of their infant are then able to accurately enough regulate their infant's emotions into optimal ranges, which then *entrains* the infant's nervous system toward optimal emotional regulation. In other words, parents' assistance in emotional regulation *becomes* the emotional regulation of the child. The world of emotional regulation is a felt, nonverbal world that is often difficult to capture in words. Yet doing so is important, as the language of the body world is what babies expect us to speak. So here are some definitions.

Synchrony

When a couple is dancing together and their movements are perfectly coordinated, their movement is in synchrony. Think professional dancers! In other words, a couple is dancing in harmony so that two people act as if they are one. They have somehow melded into one coordinated movement. They are in perfect synchrony with one another.

Resonance

Have you ever really needed to express how you were feeling and did so with a listener who was so completely in tune with you that you thought, "Wow, you get it," and this "wow" made subtle changes in your body? This may have occurred because your listener resonated with your feelings. When we feel thoroughly understood, the body communicates to us that "this is right." This is our internal guidance system speaking. You may get a feeling of relief or release, like something has been washed away, or that you suddenly have more space to breathe. When this happens, often our feelings for the listener also change. At the very least, you feel appreciative, but many times you actually feel closer to this person who has so thoroughly understood your feelings. These experiences occur in good therapy sessions. They are expressions of the body world. *Resonance* increases or amplifies feeling, and this increase has much to do with bonding to the other person.

Synchrony and resonance, then, are the molecules of attunement, and they tend to travel together. Often one will create the other. When you fall in love, for example, your feelings begin to resonate with your lover's feelings; this is generally so powerful that much of your behavior also soon falls into synchrony with your lover's, which amplifies everything! Emotional resonance has the power to create behavioral synchrony, just as behavioral synchrony can often create emotional resonance. Now how do synchrony and resonance relate to babies? Here are some examples. Do you remember what happened to you when you last heard a baby giggle?

RESONANCE CREATING SYNCHRONY: ALFONSO AND THE BALLOON

Alfonso was an adorable, good-natured, and quite robust seventeen-month-old who arrived at his aunt's birthday party with a balloon. He presented the balloon as a gift to his aunt, who accepted it graciously and clipped it onto a nearby picture frame. Shortly thereafter, Alfonso came up and batted the balloon with enough force that the clip snapped off. Alfonso started laughing, so his aunt put the clip back on. Alfonso came back, batted the balloon, and the clip fell off again. Now Alfonso was laughing hysterically—so hard, in fact, that he was practically folded in half. Alfonso did this about a hundred times with his good-natured aunt faithfully clipping the balloon to the frame again and again. What was equally wonderful was that all the adults in the room began laughing and laughing just about as hard as Alfonso. His laughter was infectious.

This led to a game of batting the balloon to Alfonso, which all the adults played when the balloon came their way. Can you see how the adults' feelings were resonant with Alfonso's emotional state and how the resonance amplified and began to bring their behavior into synchrony with his game?

For Alfonso, this game was so exciting that he was increasing or amplifying his excitement on his own. If he became tired and started to act silly because he couldn't get himself out of this state, his parents would need to help him regulate his emotions. If he didn't get tired of the balloon on his own, they could redirect him to another interesting, but perhaps lower-key, activity. His parents appeared to be feeling that some regulation was needed as his mother put a sippy cup on the coffee table and asked him if he wanted a drink. Alfonso began to wind down after he'd had a drink and didn't notice when his dad quietly moved the balloon to the next room. It worked this time likely because his parents had read his state accurately; he was getting tired. His parents actively *down-regulated* his emotional state, thereby bringing his nervous system, or the energy in his body, back into a balanced range.

There are times when parents will actively engage in increasing or *up-regulating* their baby's feelings of interest, especially when they want him to notice something. This is commonly done by a parent in a staccato voice, preceded with a big uptake of air and a pleasant startled look, used to convey a surprise. All of this increases and holds the child's attention long enough to see or experience something like, "Oh, did you hear that? Mommy is coming." In this case, parents are actively trying to increase arousal in the nervous system so that there is an increase in energy for attention.

SYNCHRONY CREATING RESONANCE: MONICA AND THE POP BEADS

Monica was a beautiful, quiet fourteen-month-old seated in the middle of the family room with her mother Jan and two sets of infant pop beads (large plastic beads that can be strung together by inserting one end into another). She sat quietly for a while before she began to pull the beads apart. Jan was mindlessly joining a few pop beads on her own and trying to catch the evening news on TV. Unbeknownst to her,

Monica stopped pulling the beads apart and began trying to join them like she had seen her mother do, but she was unsuccessful. After a little while, Jan looked up to see Monica's very sad face; Monica looked like she was about to cry. Jan asked in a gentle voice, "What's the matter, Monica?" while wondering if she was just getting tired ... maybe it was time for dinner ... possibly she needed a new toy ... but asked her if she wanted to "sit with Mommy." Jan did not really understand what caused Monica's shift toward sadness, but she resonated to Monica's feelings and used this information to synchronize her behavior toward Monica's by putting Monica in her lap. From here, Monica began to try to put the beads together, and Jan helped her. Did it matter that Jan never understood why Monica had the sad face? Not really, because she responded to her feelings, moved Monica closer, and life went on.

By resonating to Monica's feelings, Jan was able to soothe Monica even though Jan didn't catch the trigger this time. By resonating with Monica's feelings and then synchronizing her own behavior to her daughter's need (putting Monica in her lap because she looked sad), Jan reinforced their emotional connection, and this was enough. What did Monica learn? Monica was not yet old enough to think, "Gee, my mother doesn't get it," but she could feel sad because she couldn't do what her mother was doing. When Jan focused on her feelings, Monica likely had the feeling that "everything is okay now."

This is an example of attunement, misattunement, repair, and reattunement. If you are now a parent, you already know that this can occur many, many times throughout a day, let alone over an entire childhood. In fact, glitches in attunement occur throughout life and even in adult relationships! It's okay to have glitches here and there, especially when parents are sensitive enough to feel them. It is only when there is chronic misattunement without much repair that a child moves into a risk range. Can you see how Jan synchronized her behavior more toward what Monica needed, thereby reestablishing an emotional connection that likely felt resonant to both of them?

When parents synchronize their behavior with their child's while resonating with his inner feeling state, there is often a startling amplification of feeling that is not only felt within the body of both but is now shared within an *intersubjective* (knowing without words) world between the two. Try smiling at a baby. If the baby smiles back, do you have an increase in feeling? We are generally overcome with feeling! The appropriate amplification and regulation of your child's feeling states helps your child begin to regulate his emotions. It also begins to entrain your baby's nervous system to function within optimal ranges. By allowing your infant's feeling states to guide your response, you learn to accurately enough read and respond to the needs of your infant. This is the beginning of trust, upon which a secure attachment bond is established. It is also how your baby begins to feel known.

SHAPING YOUR BABY'S BRAIN

The foremost scholar to integrate the neurobiology of brain development with attachment theory is Allan Schore. Schore has made a powerful argument that early caregiver-infant interactions not only entrain the nervous system of the infant for emotional regulation but actually facilitate the structural maturation of the brain, particularly the maturation of the right hemisphere (Schore 1994). In fact, Schore's synthesis of an increasingly impressive body of research has led him to suggest that the "fundamental core of the attachment dynamic" is the parent's ability to emotionally regulate the infant's psychobiological states (Schore 1997, 600). Understanding the importance of Schore's work requires an introduction to the location and function of areas in the brain associated with secure, emotionally regulated children. This will help you see how the quality of early relationships affects brain development.

The Cerebral Hemispheres

Although the left and right hemispheres in our brain appear to be mirror images of each other, they function differently and are anatomically asymmetrical. In normal brain organization, the two hemispheres communicate together by transferring information back and forth through a thick nerve fiber called the *corpus callosum* (see figure 1). In the early work on hemisphere specialization, it was common to read books and articles referencing the right hemisphere as the nondominant, inferior, primitive, silent, and/or minor hemisphere, although it was thought to play some role in processing visual/perceptual or nonverbal material. The left was considered the dominant, superior, and/or major hemisphere,

FIGURE 1: RIGHT CEREBRAL HEMISPHERE

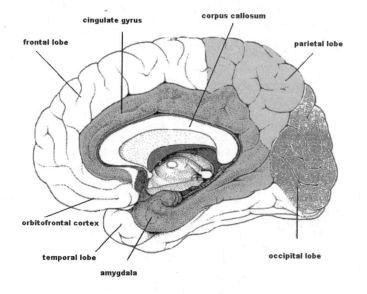

primarily because it was well known by the 1860s that damage to the left hemisphere affected the production of speech.

THE LEFT HEMISPHERE

The left hemisphere has many beauties of its own; for one, it appears to process information in a more linear fashion and, of course, allows us to speak. Groundbreaking research in the 1960s on split-brain patients, however, revealed the limitations of the left hemisphere and showed how dependent the left hemisphere was on the right hemisphere's perceptional abilities, especially the perception that builds context for verbal communication. Split-brain patients had their corpus callosum severed as a treatment for intractable epilepsy, leaving two disconnected hemispheres. Quite literally, each hemisphere functioned without the knowledge of the other. The severity of this disconnection was seen when researchers asked split-brain patients to choose a picture from an array of others to indicate a relationship to another picture they had just seen. For example, when the researchers flashed an image of a chicken claw to a patient's left hemisphere, the patient correctly chose a picture of a whole chicken. Conversely, when the researchers flashed a snow scene to the patient's right hemisphere, the patient again correctly chose a shovel. However, when the researchers later asked the patient why he had chosen these items, the patient responded, "Oh, that's simple. The chicken claw goes with the chicken, and you need a shovel to clean out the chicken shed" (Gazzaniga 1988, 13).

The patient actually created a narrative or context to explain the situation without the information known to the right hemisphere, for he was speaking out of his left hemisphere, which no longer had any connection to the right. The two hemispheres are so different, in fact, that Schore suggests that they "are two minds, two brains" that, rather than being singular entities, are in fact dual systems (Schore 2006, 13).

THE RIGHT HEMISPHERE

This simple verbal-on-the-left, nonverbal-on-the-right understanding of hemisphere specialization has dramatically given way in the face of ever-increasing research using sophisticated brain-imaging techniques that capture the brain working in real time. As it turns out, the right hemisphere appears to be the dominant hemisphere for body regulation (Schore 1994; Spence, Shapiro, and Zaidel 1996). In fact, the right hemisphere is the dominant hemisphere for the comprehension of nonverbal emotional communication, including interpreting the tones and contours of voices, faces, and gestures. It also appears to be the hemisphere that is in charge of switching problem-solving strategies based upon feedback (Kaplan and Zaidel 2001). Newer studies reveal that the right hemisphere is the dominant hemisphere for higher-level emotions such as empathy and humor. And it now appears to be critical in our having the ability to understand the mind of another human being (Saxe and Wexler 2005). In short, the right hemisphere appears to house and orchestrate the entire nonverbal body-world communication system. Without its input, our conversations are really quite meaningless.

Although our two hemispheres are connected, sometimes we too create verbal narratives that do not include the perceptions and feelings processed in our right hemispheres, that is, our bodies. The health of our own feeling worlds, our own right hemispheres, plays an important role in what babies learn about us and about their worlds. Extreme inconsistencies between what we think, feel, and say, that is, differences between our nonverbal body-world communications and our verbal stories, can be quite disorganizing to babies who are only reading our nonverbal messages in infancy.

A mother who is tired and frustrated with her baby, who is hungry, may pick up the baby and say, "I know you are hungry." You can say the words are, in fact, correct; the baby is hungry. But then add to this picture that the mother's voice is a bit sharp, her face shows tension, her eyes are averted and not looking at the baby, and her movements are abrupt, giving an overall impression that she is a bit put out at this time. So even though the mother's words have accurately identified the baby's emotional state, and she is in fact attempting to respond by feeding the baby, her own emotional communication conveys quite another story. Since babies are right-hemisphere dominant for the first three years of life (Chiron et al. 1997) and are learning and experiencing the world from a right-hemisphere perspective, what is this baby learning?

Here, the baby has two conflicting experiences. Taking in food feels good because it removes hunger, which is aversive, yet he also feels (but, of course, doesn't understand) his mother's negative feeling state. Unfortunately, if this were to chronically occur, the baby could develop the feeling that he's not worth the effort, and this would be encoded within his developing core self. Experiences like this can happen in the normal course of everyday life and could also happen with a father, but hopefully, they occur only every now and then. A chronic mismatch of caregiver communications can lead to confusion, at best, and disorganization, at worst. (As a very young child, I noticed these differences and became somewhat preoccupied with a two-person-in-one-body theory. I thought I was onto a brilliant discovery but got bogged down with a second concern: who was the real person? It probably was, however, the single-most important motivator for my becoming a psychologist.)

Rhythmic Oscillations Between the Hemispheres

Although the two hemispheres work together, the researcher Robert Thatcher found that, like a pendulum, the brain waves between the hemispheres appear to rhythmically cycle back and forth to accommodate growth spurts. He believes that these cycles occur throughout life and seem to be how the brain refines, integrates, and "sculpts" itself (Thatcher 1994). Developmental milestones, then, are directly related to the brain's growth and development.

TWO BRAINS MEET: NONVERBAL COMMUNICATION BETWEEN YOU AND YOUR BABY

Mothers tend to hold their babies on their left side (baby's head on mother's left arm). Take a look. In fact, about 83 percent of right-handed mothers and 78 percent of left-handed mothers cradle their babies on the left (Sieratzki and Woll 1996). This has also been found to be true for fathers. Monkeys and apes also have been found to cradle their young on the left. When you see a behavior in the animal kingdom rolling over into humans, suspect nature has a really good reason for that behavior. The way the visual system is organized, what is seen in the left visual field projects directly to the right hemisphere before crossing the corpus callosum (conversely, what is seen in the right visual field projects directly to the left hemisphere before crossing over). Cradling your baby on the left places your baby's right hemisphere in direct communication with your right hemisphere. This is the beginning of right-hemisphere-to-right-hemisphere conversations, using the ancient and intimate language of faces, eyes, tones of voice, touch, and gestures; it is also the beginning of one brain imprinting another (Schore 1994).

One important reason (there are many) to breastfeed a baby is for both the mother and baby to have these intimate nonverbal conversations. To the outer world, this may simply look like a mother nursing her baby. In the body world of nursing, however, the mother's and child's body interiors can come into synchrony with one another. This feels great to both mother and baby, especially if the mother just allows herself to relax and enjoy this intimacy. (Not all mothers are able to breastfeed, or they do not enjoy breastfeeding. You can still feel this intimacy if you hold your baby in your arms while bottle-feeding and let yourself sink into your feelings.) I cannot say enough about how important it is for both mother and father to sink into the body feelings of your babies. How this all feels to the baby is what goes into the quality of the baby's attachment to you. Remember that the attachment bond is forming not specifically because the baby is being fed. Being fed feels good with milk in the tummy, but this is quite secondary to the nourishment your baby receives through the love he sees in your eyes or the feeling of protection he experiences while you hold him closely. This is attunement. All rhythms are rocking together. It won't happen every time, but if it happens enough, a secure bond will be well on its way. Although science rarely uses the word "love," attunement surely is associated with love and caring, and it certainly is intimate.

Attunement in Your Daily Lives

As you know by now, improved parent attunement positively affects the quality of a child's attachment to his parents and provides feelings of security. Indeed, increased attunement in all of our relationships tends to improve the quality of our relationships, but the young child requires attunement to develop. In our time, family life has become increasingly complex and demanding, which, for some, will make attuning to your child quite a challenge. As the psychology supervisor for St. Vincent de Paul Village, a center for homeless adults and families with children, I train interns to read the nonverbal interactions between children and parents to identify possible problems in parent-child attunement, and to provide interventions to improve the parents' ability to understand their young child's communications.

This is not easy work with all that goes into homelessness, but I am always delighted when my interns come to the conclusion that "you really can read the nonverbal language of the child." And not only that, but you can read any child, no matter when they were born or what culture they were born into. That's because babies are babies across culture and time, and they all start out speaking the ancient, universal language of the body. I find this reassuring and personally hold the hope that what might connect us all will be found in the care and understanding of babies, that is, the body world before concepts take root.

So being able to move into the nonverbal world of young children, or becoming more right-hemisphere dominant on demand, so to speak, is critical. This can present challenges for all of us, depending upon our life circumstances. It can be particularly challenging for working parents with demanding, detail-oriented, left-brain careers or with jobs that are physically demanding. Demanding careers naturally create fatigue that requires restorative time. Some parents find their children a source of restoration and can't wait to get home. Others need a little time to themselves. Meanwhile, stay-at-home parents who have been in their young child's nonverbal, preverbal, or barely verbal world may be eager for some adult interactions. I will talk more about these issues in the next chapter, but for now, here's a look at what it means to make time to tune in to your child.

SHIFTING TO THE RIGHT: MAKING TIME TO TUNE IN TO YOUR CHILD

So how do we shift out of our left-brain, detail-oriented worlds and slip into a child's world enough to be attuned? There is no magical switch for choosing hemispheres like you find in cars for adjusting left and right mirrors; the hemispheres are built to transfer information across the corpus callosum automatically. However, your own early experiences and current life can affect how flexible you are in shifting from the verbal to the body world of the child.

A Two-Professional Home with Two Children Under Five: The Hatch Family

Annette and Howard Hatch were both professionals with high-powered, demanding careers. They had two children: Jake, an adorable four-year-old who liked to move, and Jessica, an equally adorable one-year-old who seemed to giggle at the sight of her brother. Jessica could be a bit hesitant when she engaged with people she didn't know and needed time to warm up. Annette's professional career demanded after-hour preparation that could extend into the night. Howard's profession allowed for more consistent nonworking home time. After Annette found out she was pregnant with Jake, Annette and Howard had operated as one unit with Howard attending most if not all prenatal visits, birthing classes, and the birth. The same was true when Jessica was born. Both children were in child care and had been since early infancy. Annette and Howard had both researched local child care programs until they felt secure with the quality and care of one that they selected close to their home. Since Annette was typically less available by phone than Howard, he was usually the contact person for the child care center. Annette rearranged her schedule to be more available by phone when Howard was out of town.

In the Hatch family living room sat a large tub filled with toys for Jessica and Jake. More often, the toys were scattered across the floor leaving traces of previous play. There was a toy basketball hoop in the dining room with a ball lying under the table. Dishes from the morning were piled up on the counter, and there was a large black bag of trash filling up alongside. Howard had picked up the children from child care, and they were starting dinner. Annette was feeding Jessica in her high chair with wide-eyed, animated expressions that made Jessica smile. Howard was fixing dinner while talking with Jake, who was pushing two noisy trucks around the kitchen floor. In the bedroom, Annette had files stacked about a foot high that had to be reviewed that evening. Jake pulled up to his mom to talk about a friend in child care who took his toy, how he told the teacher, and she got it back. Annette and Howard praised him while exchanging meaningful looks, remembering his first and only incident report last year when another child had taken his toy and he had responded with a bite.

Annette calmly changed places with Howard, who began to feed Jessica, who was now wearing a lot of food and smiling at her dad. Jessica was busy picking up pieces of food from her tray when Jake came up to give her a tremendous hug that significantly adjusted her seating. Howard readjusted her, calmly commenting, "Careful, Jake." Jessica was now smiling from ear to ear as she usually does when just seeing Jake. Next, Annette set the table, Jessica's high chair was pulled around to face the table, and in a few minutes the family sat down together and ate. This family might take a walk to the nearby park with the children after dinner, or one parent might flop down on the sofa or floor with the children while the other started to clean the kitchen. Bedtime routines were also divided, and by eight or eight-thirty, Howard usually collapsed in front of the TV to watch a movie while Annette reviewed her files. This occurred most evenings.

Annette and Howard were consistently responsive to their children. They were also remarkably calm parents even though they had their normal moments of irritation. At family gatherings, they could easily leave adult conversation to attend to the children. And they could do so with both the adult and their child in mind. For example, knowing that Jessica was a bit shy around newcomers, Howard came over right away to help Jessica stay calm when I approached her to say good-bye. Howard kept her emotions within a comfortable range by moving closer to her and providing a mini-step (scaffolding) for her by saying, "Say 'bye-bye,' Jessica," something she knew how to say. Howard turned this moment of potential guardedness for Jessica and perhaps awkwardness for me to a fun *I know how to do this* moment where everyone was successful. Do you see how this was similar to what Kyle's mother did? This was an incredibly attuned interaction to two emotional states, his daughter's and a guest's.

Despite their heavy work schedules, Annette and Howard were managing to create a secure world for their children. As Annette recently said, "We are exhausted, but the children are doing great." That's how it looked to me too. In case you are wondering how two professionals could possibly make dinner after a full day's work with bedtime routines looming ahead, the Hatches were quite comfortable with getting takeout; in fact, they could give you a fairly good account of the local restaurants that have family-friendly menus.

The Hatch parents also physically moved closer to their children when they needed stimulation or soothing. Too often, comfortably seated, tired parents hope that "explaining in words" will be enough to regulate or soothe their children. It won't. In fact, it will make matters worse as the young child, even preschoolers, are still reading the tone and rhythm of voice, facial expressions, and body distance of the parent as their primary language. Here's an example.

Leif's Hurt Arm

While waiting for a prescription in a crowded clinic pharmacy, everyone looked up at a mother who was using a rather loud teaching voice to explain to her young child how he must monitor the swelling in his arm and "let me know immediately if it gets bigger, because if it increases in size it can be a dangerous condition that will require Mommy to bring you back to the hospital." This went on for about five minutes. Leif, who looked upset anyway, was now slipping down out of the chair away from his mother, looking at his arm, and trying to suppress tears. What a confusing and frightening interaction for him. In the world of attachment, this is not a sensitive, attuned response to a young child. If Leif's mother had been able to attune to her child's internal state, she would have known that he was scared and likely in pain too. Holding him close using a softer, more intimate voice, and saying something like "it will be okay; we'll watch it [the swelling]" is much more soothing and helps a child regain balance and a sense of safety. This would also bring his nervous system back into a more normal range. It was interesting to watch the other people in the waiting room, who were exchanging looks. People were visibly uncomfortable hearing this mother, as our own right minds felt the misattunement. Although it was clear that Leif's mother was worried about him, it was equally clear that she was stuck in her own left-brain world, so to speak, and could not shift to the right.

So what have you learned? You have learned that secure attachment is directly related to attunement and attunement is related to the right hemisphere. You have also learned that, when needed, amplifying (up-regulating) and/or down-regulating your child's feeling states leads to emotional regulation, which is highly associated with secure attachment. Why? Because these parent-child experiences begin to entrain your baby's autonomic nervous system to function within optimal ranges. This is called *interactive regulation*, where the parent is *co-regulating* the child's emotions by understanding his feelings through attunement. Children need their parents' help in regulating their emotions until they are able to do so themselves. This is called *self-regulation*. When sensitive parents consistently enough help their children regulate their emotions within optimal ranges, children act and feel more confident, show greater competence at exploring and learning about their worlds, and learn to regulate their emotions themselves.

Now it's time to head back to the world of the brain.

HELPING YOUR CHILD PASS THROUGH THE SURVIVAL GATES

The brain has evolved over millions of years based upon experience. Therefore, it should be no surprise that actual experience affects the brain. Nature is quite invested in making sure we have the equipment needed to survive our environments and, over time, has continually refined the structure of the brain.

The Amygdala

The *amygdala* is one of our oldest monitoring structures (see figure 1), located deep within a part of the brain called the *limbic system* which includes more complex structures that integrate incoming information from sight, sound, smell, touch, and movement. The limbic system is particularly sensitive to emotional processing and memory. The amygdala is a subcortical structure that is especially sensitive to information that falls within a threat range, so it will fire if we are in fear; it is also involved when we are angry. It is a crude regulatory system that appraises the external environment for threats to survival and is capable of commanding the autonomic nervous system for this use. The amygdala is like a watchdog monitoring the environment for threats, and if it senses one, it can trigger the sympathetic and parasympathetic branches of the nervous system, which control the energy levels in our bodies.

The Sympathetic and Parasympathetic Nervous Systems

The *sympathetic nervous system* (SNS) increases heart rate, blood pressure, respiration, and temperature needed to prepare the body for physical and/or mental activity. It is always activated during times of stress, emotional expression, and/or threat. Activation in response to threat prepares the body for a defensive response like fight or flight. Moderate levels of SNS activation, however, are needed for work, play, and exploration. The *parasympathetic nervous system* (PNS) tries to balance the activation of the SNS by putting brakes on activation for energy restoration and is considered the balancing agent of the autonomic nervous system. The PNS lowers blood pressure, heart rate, respiration, and temperature to reduce SNS activation; it is involved in sleep. The PNS can also be involved in defense, for it can dramatically put the body into a freeze response, feigning death as a means of protection. Flight, fight, and freeze responses are controlled by the amygdala to keep us alive if we're threatened.

The Orbitofrontal Cortex

A newer part of the brain, the *cortex*, is thought to have developed about 300 million years ago and to have increased in size about 1.5 million years ago (Carter 1998). The front part of the brain, called the *frontal cortex* or *lobes*, contains an area that has been found to be critical in the regulation of emotion and attention. This area, which is located behind and slightly above the eyes, is called the *orbitofrontal cortex* (see figure 1). The orbitofrontal cortex in the right hemisphere has direct connections to the autonomic nervous system and can assert control over the more reactive subcortical regions. There are two important regulatory circuits that connect this part of the brain to the subcortical areas: one is *excitatory*, is associated with positive emotional states, and is controlled by the sympathetic nervous system; the other is *inhibitory*, is associated with negative emotional states, and is controlled by the parasympathetic nervous system. When these two regulatory circuits are optimally functioning and balanced more toward positive emotions, the higher regulatory centers have greater influence over the more primitive appraisals of the amygdala (Schore 1994, 2001a). The amygdala, however, still has the ability to override even a well-connected higher regulatory structure if we are confronted with a life-threatening danger.

Interactive Regulation, Attunement, and the Amygdala

The secure young child has enough interactive regulation from sensitive enough parents to settle the amygdala down. In other words, if a child is startled or afraid, the parent will help the child regulate his emotions while providing needed scaffolding so that he can get past his fear. Kyle's mother, for example, actively moved his nervous system past the amygdala and kept his arousal within a range that did not interfere with his learning how to ride a wave. The insecure-avoidant child, however, has been entrained to not have or show feelings because his parents tend to dismiss feelings in favor of being a "big boy." Parents of avoidant children chronically deactivate their attachment system, thereby leaving the child in a *hypoaroused* state, that is, a nonoptimal low-energy state that interferes with learning and exploration, at least when with the parent. This is difficult for two reasons: one, there has been too little sensitive interactive regulation to settle the amygdala down, so it will continue to fire whenever the child is afraid or angry (which can be often if no one helps you understand how the world works); and two, the child's nervous system is in a double bind. On the one hand, the avoidant child is encouraged to put the brakes on his emotions, stressing the parasympathetic nervous system, yet nature is pushing him to explore and grow, which requires the sympathetic nervous system. This may be why multiple studies are finding increased aggression in avoidant children, as over time this tension in the nervous system needs to be released. Lastly, the insecure-ambivalent child, who never knows if his caregiver will be available, has a hyperactivated attachment system, corresponding with high SNS activation, which can greatly interfere with exploration. This child is *hyperaroused* most of the time, for his strategy produces anger, anxiety, and vigilance. With this child, the amygdala is likely to be very reactive, as he does not experience consistent-enough interactive regulation.

BUILDING REGULATED BRAINS: HOW PARENTS HELP

There is one last area of brain development that you need to know about, which is how your interactions with your baby are associated with neuronal growth. Babies are born with 100 billion neurons in their brains, all ready for connections. It's as if Mother Nature said, "Here, I'll provide as many flexible blocks as I can and even color code them somewhat, so you can arrange them to fit your environment, your culture, your time, and your interests. Later I'll remove any you aren't using to give you more space."

Neurons: Brain Fibers That Organize Information into Networks

Neurons are communicating fibers that carry information. Like developing trees, neurons sprout branches called *dendrites* so that more information can be received. When a critical mass of information is received, the neuron reaches an electrical threshold that propels the information down its output channel, called an *axon*, and releases a *neurotransmitter* (biochemical) into a space called a *synapse*. As the neurotransmitter drifts across this space, a receiving dendrite picks up the charge and the process repeats. Cell growth proliferates in the first years of life. By three years of age, the child has about 1,000 trillion synapses (Balbernie 2001). In healthy babies, a natural pruning of excessive cells occurs that fine-tunes and strengthens the connections that fit the infant's environment (de Graaf-Peters and Hadders-Algra 2006; Schore 2001a). When abuse and neglect occur in the infant's caregiving environment, increased levels of stress hormones can induce cell death and cause brain atrophy (Balbernie 2001; Schore 1994, 2001b). When the cell pruning occurs in this situation, it can leave the child with a lack of needed connections and/or disorganized and chaotic circuitry in the brain.

Neural Networks: The Organization of Neurons

Patterns of neuronal growth, called *neural networks*, connect and communicate to areas of the brain with lightning speed. Because neural growth and patterns are mirroring experience, lived experience is actually encoding and entraining the brain's neural circuits and systems throughout the genetically driven sensitive periods of development. Developmental experiences are etched into the brain, producing a unique pattern of neural networks based upon the entwining of genetics and experience. A child's internal working model (see chapter 1) appears to be related to the organization of this genetic-experience system in the brain, which grows into personality and gives us a sense of self (Damasio 1999; Schore 1994). Efficient travel through well-developed neural networks into higher brain centers allows the child to access the more advanced regulatory systems in the brain. You can begin to see more cortical emotional control in two-year-old Asia, when she asked her grandmother to find her favorite child program on TiVo. After watching her grandmother struggling with various remotes and numerous buttons, she said, "You're not very good at this, Grandma," but continued to wait patiently. When Grandma did manage to find the program, Asia patted her on the shoulder and said, "You did good!" This is an example of higher cortical regulation in a young child and is quite different from a child who starts to get frustrated and angry, and perhaps even throws a tantrum because the program is not forthcoming.

Fueling the Brain: How Attunement Creates Biochemicals Needed for Growth

Infants love face-to-face social interaction, particularly the faces of their parents. As development proceeds, infants begin to explore objects and others in their environments with equal excitement. In highly intense social face-to-face interactions, parents will actively increase their infant's emotions to joy states, where everyone now has a cascade of endorphins flowing through their bodies. Daniel Stern (1985) calls these mutual states of pleasure *vitality affects*, that is, explosive feelings of aliveness that are created by the shared parent and child experience. The resulting resonance does three important things: it increases pleasurable biochemicals in the child's brain, thereby strengthening neural pathways associated with pleasure and motivation; it strengthens the parent's bond to the baby and the baby's attachment bond to the parent; and it begins to form that "knowing without words" world of intersubjectivity, or "we" world, between the two.

Sensitive Periods for Brain Development: Pregnancy and the First Three Years of Life

Although development occurs throughout life, the overarching sensitive period for sculpting and connecting the right hemisphere needed to support the emergent self starts in pregnancy and continues with great force throughout the first three years of life. This time period is critical for the neurobiological health of children. It is so critical, in fact, that there is an urgent need for greater societal understanding of this developmental period and support for parents raising young children.

While the basic wiring of the brain is influenced by genetics, which guides the unfolding of development in a stage-by-stage fashion during sensitive periods, there is an increasing understanding that it is the infant's environmental experience that provides the needed fuel or energy for brain maturation. Just as food and sleep are needed for growth and development, infant emotional regulation is associated with optimal levels of facilitating biochemicals in the brain to stimulate and organize neural growth and connectivity and maintain neurobiological balance (Schore 1994, 1997). In fact, emotional regulation of the nervous system (and all that this means to brain development) is what's going on behind the face. When parents are attuned enough, they play a critical role in regulating their baby's autonomic nervous system as they enhance positive emotions while regulating negative emotions.

Again, Parents Only Have to Be Good Enough

Infant-parent face-to-face research done by Ed Tronick, Beatrice Beebe, Tiffany Field, Ruth Feldman, and others, using second-by-second time series analyses, shows us who is doing what and when in the attunement dance. Using two cameras, one focused on the infant and the other on the parent, these researchers provide a clearer picture of how parents regulate their infants' emotional states, but they also show just how much infants affect their parents' behavior. Young infants have many feeling states. They can be in a quiet alert state, an intense social interaction that is filled with smiling, cooing, and sometimes giggling, or they can be in a drowsy don't-bother-me state, a distressed and fussing state, or a generally unhappy-until-something-is-adjusted state. Infants can also signal when they are overaroused and need a break. New parents are not only learning about feeding, changing diapers, adjusting temperature, and infant sleep rhythms, they are also learning to adjust their own voices, visual expressions, holding positions, and their own sleep rhythms, to keep their child within optimal emotional ranges. Luckily, nature has a built-in signal to guide us quickly into trying to figure it all out: crying!

Parents are able to make their way through infant regulation using their own instincts and feelings ... and the advice of a good pediatrician. Infant researchers have helped us see that mothers regulate their babies by altering their own emotional intensity, facial expressions, response timing, visual gazing, and the contours, pitch, and rhythm of their voices in response to their infant's internal states (Beebe and Lachmann 2002; Field 1985; Stern 1985). And guess what? Dads can do this too.

Fathers Are Needed in Emotional Regulation

It is now known that fathers can attune to their infant just as well as mothers can, though their pattern of infant interaction is often different. Ruth Feldman (2003) did a second-by-second time series, face-to-face analysis on firstborn infants with both parents and found that both mothers and fathers could match their infant's emotional or feeling states. She showed that mothers generally used more rhythmic dialogue with low-to-moderate emotional expression, thought to not only imitate the sounds and feelings of intrauterine life but to also introduce the rhythm of future social dialogue. Feldman also found a thought-provoking interaction. Same-gender dyads, that is, mothers with female infants and fathers with male infants, had better emotional matching and shorter response lags than did opposite-gender pairs. Feldman wonders if there is a unique biologically driven need for the same-gendered parent in emotional regulation, particularly, as she points out, given the literature associating father absence with emotional dysregulation.

The shape of healthy interactive emotional regulation appears to be that either the infant or his parent can seek the other's attention, with parents exaggerating their vocal and facial responses to support the infant's increasing positive emotions. And conversely, either infant or parent can disengage from interactions by reducing emotional intensity through changes in the face and voice, including gaze aversion, voice changes, and/or turning away. It is only when babies are chronically in high (hyperaroused) or low (hypoaroused) emotional states for long periods of time, as a result of parental misattunements that are inadequately repaired, that defensive strategies begin to develop. For babies experiencing traumatic relationships fraught with fear, pain, abuse, or neglect, with little to no positive interactions, the amygdala can seize control of the autonomic nervous system to auto-regulate the body.

The Effects of Trauma on Brain Development

Although this book is not about trauma in particular, it is important for parents to have some familiarity with the growing body of research studying the effects of trauma on the brain, particularly its dysregulation of the right hemisphere (Schore 2002, 2003). It is now well known that a history of trauma, including attachment trauma, affects multiple brain sites and the ability to regulate emotions during stress. In the early years of development, the experience of trauma, abuse, and neglect can strengthen the firing of the amygdala so much that this experience is, in effect, "burnt in" (Stuss and Alexander 1999) to the amygdala. This experience hampers the development of neural connections to higher right-brain regulatory structures (capable of mediating the amygdala response). In particular, the amygdala in the right hemisphere is thought to play a critical role in modulating emotions; given the amygdala's primitive memory capability, some believe it plays an important role in implicit memory. *Implicit memory* is a nonconscious memory system that guides behavior beneath conscious awareness, like riding a bike. Mancia (2006) believes implicit memory holds the "sensory presymbolic and preverbal experiences of the infant" that are colored by positive or negative emotional experiences given by the parent. Because of implicit memory's presymbolic origins, Mancia describes a "kind of memory [that] cannot in fact be remembered" (93).

This idea has tremendous importance, for it suggests that nonverbal, presymbolic, right-hemisphere memory structures are encoding feeling states that cannot be verbalized or accessed through a conscious process. The ambient experiences of emotions in the home (smiling, as opposed to harsh or flat faces; gentle touch, as opposed to rough or little touch; laughing, soft and animated voices, as opposed to sharp, frustrated, or loud voices; and/or waiting too long for someone to respond, as opposed to sensitive responding) may be encoded in this system. This may help explain how adult attachment categories can so robustly predict infant attachment categories over time.

59

EMOTIONAL REGULATION AND DYSREGULATION: CASE EXAMPLES

Consider the following three young children in terms of emotional regulation, emotional dysregulation, misattunement, and repair.

Emotional Dysregulation/Hyperarousal: Phillip

Phillip was a handsome thirteen-month-old whom I noticed while boarding a plane heading to Hawaii. Prior to getting on the plane, Phillip began screaming while walking with his mother and his five-year-old sister. Phillip's father was walking quite a bit ahead of Phillip's mother and the children, so far ahead, in fact, that it was hard to know that they were connected. In the meantime, Phillip screamed and cried all the way to the gate. On the plane, he continued to scream and cry in his seat with his mother for two hours. He was very, very distressed, so much so that the people in the surrounding seats were distressed (as, by then, all of our attachment systems were now activated). Phillip's mother could not soothe him. When she tried to rock him, he screamed more. Singing to him produced greater distress. She tried to get him to lie down in her seat while she sat on the floor. She laid her head on his stomach, perhaps thinking of a nice kissing-the-stomach game (or perhaps she was simply exhausted), but he screamed even louder. At one point, she made the rather dubious decision of putting Phillip on the floor under her feet, but to Phillip's credit, he took the opportunity to crawl out and head down the aisle; absolutely no crying. His mother followed him down the aisle, picked him up, and walked with him up on her shoulder…not a peep. And then the "fasten seat belt" sign went on … alas, what a pity for this mom and baby (and all of us), because as soon as his mother sat down, Phillip began to scream again.

Feeling sad (and frustrated) for both Phillip and his mother, I started to wonder about the effect this level of dysregulation had on his mother's feeling of competency and Phillip's well-being. As I was contemplating ways I might help the mother, Phillip escaped again, but this time, he pulled up to the man directly across the aisle from the mother and was picked up! This was Dad. Phillip collapsed on his father, and fell asleep, and there was not another sound heard from him for the remainder of the flight.

We would all agree, Phillip was emotionally dysregulated. His sympathetic nervous system was hyperactivated and had been for a long time. Although his mother attempted to soothe him, she could not reduce his arousal. She tried a variety of approaches, but still she couldn't regulate his distress. You could say that Phillip's mother was misattuned in that Phillip was signaling distress and she couldn't figure out what he needed, or perhaps she knew what he needed but was horribly constrained for reasons that may or may not be obvious. In fact, her attempts at soothing seemed to increase his distress. Only when he crawled off or when he was at her shoulder did he stop crying, which is a clue. Letting Phillip go or giving him more space, that is, *not* interacting with him, was what soothed his distress and would have likely repaired the misattunement.

Babies this age do signal when enough is enough, and they do need disengagement, at times, to recover. In fact, if a parent has covered all other fronts—hunger, diaper change, pain or illness, and so on—high arousal states can be from fatigue alone, which may require modulated disengagement in preparation for sleep. For Phillip, the repair occurred through his father, who did not engage Phillip at all, and Phillip promptly fell asleep.

Of course, a few things stand out here. What personal issues were involved for these parents, we will never know. Clearly, however, their lack of communication with each other was at Phillip's expense. Phillip's mother and father did not show signs of attunement to each other and/ or did not respond to each other for other relationship reasons, even when their child was in distress. Again, there may be a natural same-gender advantage for emotional regulation (Feldman 2003), and Phillip may have wanted and needed his father. What Phillip learned, though, was that his father *would not* respond to him, even when he was upset, for reasons that he could not possibly understand. If the family interacts this way all the time, Phillip is learning that he must be extremely upset for long periods of time, to the point of exhaustion, before his father will respond. As Phillip grows and develops, this kind of interaction will be confusing for him to understand and may affect his developing sense of self. Certainly, it is the father's needs here (whatever they may be) that are being met ... not Phillip's.

Emotional Dysregulation/Hypoarousal: Emma

Emma was a lovely two-year-old girl living at St. Vincent's with her mother and other siblings. Emma was evaluated in our young child program. She was very bright, yet she rarely smiled and had poor eye contact. Although her mother loved her, she tended to speak harshly to Emma. Emma never looked at or approached her mother during the hour-long evaluation, even when tired. During the evaluation, she presented her accomplishments to the evaluator instead of to her mother. Emma also attended the licensed child care program at St. Vincent's, while her mother took classes in preparation for work. She had received numerous incident reports for aggression, including biting, hitting, screaming, and angry outbursts. The child care teachers noted that she did better one-on-one with an adult; when she was with other children, Emma became aggressive.

Emma had learned to hold her feelings in or avoid them and tried to focus on her budding intellect as her mother praised her for being smart. In fact, Emma's mother encouraged her to help with the care of her new four-month-old sister though Emma was only two.

Avoiding feelings at any age is not recommended, as feeling is the language of our bodies, and a two-year-old's very existence is feeling. Her mother's rejection of Emma's feelings could become encoded for Emma as a rejection of her very self. Since rejection of self leads to shame (and heartbreak), a child will typically develop some kind of defensive strategy, and Emma was developing an avoidant strategy. Rather than express her needs to her mother, she tried to have no needs. Clearly, however, she didn't have the regulatory capacity to be successful. In the presence of her mother, she was able to exert inhibitory control, but when she was on a child care site interacting with the normal push-and-pull of toddlers, she broke down into aggression and negativity.

Emma didn't know how to interact with other children because she'd had so little interactive regulation with her mother. On the one hand, Emma was underaroused for healthy exploration; on the other hand, she was quite dysregulated on the child care site. Her mother actively reinforced Emma's control of her emotions when they were together, thereby stressing the parasympathetic branch of her nervous system at the expense of increasing arousal needed for play and exploration.

Emotional Regulation: Sarah

Sarah was a beautiful, big-eyed fourteen-month-old infant, also flying to Hawaii with her mother. Sarah was crawling around on one of the seats next to her mother; they had two seats at the back of the plane. During several of my walks (it's a long flight), she greeted me with a toothy smile. As I smiled back, she giggled, then I laughed, and suddenly we were having a fabulous conversation. Sarah's mother was smiling at us; she seemed calm, open, and friendly. I commented on what a wonderful baby she had, and she nodded and said, "She likes you." I could feel the mother-infant bubble of their connection, and now I'd been invited into their bubble. I felt happy to have seen them and returned to my seat with this happiness in my heart. I imagined their lives as contented with a mother feeling competent with her baby. Sarah was emotionally regulated. She felt free to explore what interested her within the safety of her mother's protection. Sarah could greet and be curious about someone new who talked with her as she felt her mother's attunement signaling that this interaction was okay.

WIRING OPTIMAL AROUSAL RANGES INTO THE AUTONOMIC NERVOUS SYSTEM

Parents who respond sensitively to their infant's arousal states are, in fact, entraining flexible ranges and optimal levels of activation into their child's autonomic nervous system. Parents of secure children respond quickly to negative emotions that are stressful to everyone, thereby helping to reduce the stress hormones in their child's body. They also enhance positive emotions through play, thereby increasing positive biochemicals used for neuronal growth and brain maturation. Secure children learn to self-regulate their emotions because they have had parents to help them regulate.

Sarah, for one, was free to explore her environment and interact with others, while her mother sat nearby. And I feel quite certain that had Sarah had a fuss on the plane for some reason, her mother would have responded to her in a way that would help calm her. This attunement feels to babies like *life is okay, safe and secure, and I can't wait until the next moment when something else wonderful will happen.* Sarah was likely a secure baby, whose mother actively kept her internal physiology within an optimal range by sensitively enhancing positive emotional states and regulating negative emotional ones. This tipping-toward-positive emotions balances the body and provides the right biochemical mix used to explore and learn.

IN A NUTSHELL: REGULATE NEGATIVE EMOTIONS WHILE ENHANCING POSITIVE EMOTIONS

CHAPTER 3

Crossing into a New Ocean:

Pregnancy, Birth, and the Newborn Period

*A hundred years from now, it will not matter what my
bank account was, the sort of house I lived in, or the
make of car I drove. But the world may be different,
because I was important in the life of a child.*
—author unknown

Creating babies in moments of passion can be very sexy between lovers
who are not focused on the next morning. Yet the next morning does come
and often with what seems like instant subtle body changes in a future
mother. As the future dad rolls out of bed looking for the paper, the future
mom may be privately calculating the date of her last period. Throughout
history, making babies has defied birth control, age, cultural expectations,

and time primarily because sexual attraction is instinctual and powered by nature, which wants those genes transferred. Whether or not we are prepared to have the evidence of our private sexual moments made public, however, is another story. Yet those wide-eyed smiling bundles of truth arrive carrying the genetic material of their biological parents.

Luckily, for most couples, becoming pregnant is either a planned event or an acceptable surprise within a stable marriage or relationship. For first-time parents, it will be a time full of new questions as well. This chapter will talk about the psychological changes that occur in pregnancy that begin to prepare you for bonding with your baby. Pregnancy is a time when wider rings of social structure begin to light up suddenly, often in a startling way. Pregnancy has a way of bringing families of origin closer together. For most couples, this is a healthy and exciting process, but it can be a challenging time too as couples are not only adjusting their own relationship boundaries to include their new baby but are also establishing their new family within the larger social context of extended family and friends.

Having a child changes your life. It also changes the form of your life. You are no longer solely an individual or a couple, but you are each also now someone's mother or father. The birth of a family brings additional twists and turns in the psychology of individuals and couples. Like a volcano, birth is an eruption of life from which the terrain is permanently changed. In this chapter, I will focus on this great transition of pregnancy, birth, and the first eight weeks of life as it relates to attachment and affect regulation.

SETTING THE SCENE: THE TRANSITION TO PARENTHOOD

The Panama Canal is a remarkable engineering feat connecting the Atlantic and Pacific oceans, creating an 8,000-mile shortcut for a ship traveling from New York to San Francisco. Ships can enter from either the Atlantic or Pacific. Upon entering the canal, a ship has to travel across a series of locks before entering Gatun Lake, which is 85 feet above sea level. After it crosses the lake, the ship is then lowered through another series of locks to sea level again and into the other ocean. Once a ship enters the lock, it begins a continuous course that guides the ship to the other side ... there is no turning back.

So goes pregnancy. Once pregnant, the body world takes over, bringing on different body changes and feelings throughout the three trimesters. Just when a couple believes they have mastered one set of changes, another arrives. And this continues until the baby is born … and then, of course, a new set of changes arises. Like the ship that enters the Panama Canal to get to the other ocean, a couple enters the approach channel of pregnancy as two individuals riding together, and they arrive on the other side as a family. During the passage, they accomplish many physical and psychological changes. The physical changes are quite obvious. What is less obvious are the psychological and interpersonal adjustments needed to widen the relationship to include a new baby. What is equally less noticeable is that your own emotional regulation histories seem to resurface when babies are around.

MARRIAGES, COMMITMENTS, AND OTHER NECESSARY INGREDIENTS

It is well known that the quality of the marriage or commitment that parents have to each other affects the developing child. In fact, conflict between parents is associated with greater conflict between parents and their kids (Fincham 1998). Conversely, happy and fulfilling marriages or partnerships are associated with less parent-child conflict. The fact that your relationship with your partner affects your child is not hard to understand if you consider that conflict between couples generally includes angry exchanges that babies may register as frightening and unsafe. Conversely, parents who are affectionate and treat each other with kindness, dishing out healthy doses of smiling, laughter, and warmth, emanate good feelings and create an ambience that babies register as safe, interesting, and playful.

Father Involvement: Father's Important Role

Fathers are incredibly important to babies. Fathers can diaper, feed, hold, rock, play with, talk to, and attune to their babies just as mothers can. In fact, as mentioned in chapter 2, fathers have a unique regulatory rhythm for children, especially for baby boys (Feldman 2003) that may be biological. The father is also the other half of the couple who produced this baby and will hopefully go to all the prenatal appointments and birthing classes and be present at birth, whether formally married to the baby's mother or not.

Father involvement in the transition to parenthood is highly associated with how sensitive a mother will be with the baby (Feldman 2000) and to her satisfaction in the marriage (Shapiro, Gottman, and Carrere 2000). Meanwhile, multiple studies show that fathers' sensitivity to and involvement with infants is dependent upon the quality of their marriage/relationship. In fact, the most consistent predictor of father involvement with the newborn is marital/relationship happiness (Feldman, Nash, and Aschenbrenner 1983). This all means that raising a baby together in a happy enough relationship will likely be satisfying for everyone concerned. Being able to know how each other is feeling, that is, attuning to each other, is as important to raising babies as it is to happy relationships. Staying attuned enough to each other will help you make this special passage, raise a secure child, and stretch your relationship boundaries to include your new baby without too much fuss.

Putting this together then, the more intimate and confiding a couple's personal relationship, the more likely it is that the father will be involved with the baby's care. The more the father is involved in the baby's care, the more likely it is that the mother will be able to be sensitive and attuned to the baby (Cox et al. 1989; Feldman 2000). This is how the quality of the couple's relationship directly translates to parental sensitivity, which leads to attunement and emotional regulation in the baby. What seems to protect a couple's relationship through the transition into parenthood is continuing access to the original, prior-to-baby relationship and the couple's commitment to each other.

IT REALLY DOES TAKE A VILLAGE: YOUR SUPPORT SYSTEM

Babies are born into increasingly complex environments. Sometimes prior-to-baby adult relationships include other children from previous relationships, parenting commitments with divorced biological parents who are no longer in the home, and/or a new relationship commitment with someone who is now a stepmother or stepfather. Prior-to-baby relationships generally include grandparents and friends as well. In fact, family configurations are typically different from what they were thirty years ago. What may seem surprising is that the 2002 U.S. Census Bureau shows that only 24 percent of the households with children consisted of married couples with only their own biological children (Fields and Casper 2001). This leaves a wide range for other family configurations, including children living in married two-parent blended families, in single-parent homes with or without a cohabiting partner, in grandparent or other relative homes, or in same-sex partner homes. There is also evidence that the quality of a future mother's relationship to her own mother (maternal grandmother) is important, for one study following three generations clearly shows that the maternal grandmother's attachment category predicted the mother's attachment category, which, in turn, predicted her infant's attachment category (Benoit and Parker 1994).

Now add the fact that in many households, both parents have to work. In fact, of children living in two-parent homes, 62 percent have both parents in the workforce, 30 percent have stay-at-home mothers, and 4 percent have stay-at-home fathers (Fields 2003). Some parents have careers requiring long hours to stay competitive, most have financial obligations, and others have work lives that require the ongoing monitoring of multiple details, which can be draining. Even for a stay-at-home mom or dad running a house, getting children to and from events, arranging playdates, fixing meals, responding, responding, responding, can be exhausting. Knowing your own needs for regulation will greatly help establish the right household routine for you and your new family.

Creating a support system for pregnancy, birth, and your child's development is critical both for the adults who are the primary attachment figures and for the baby. In two-parent homes, the parents can share the special and intimate experience of caring for their child together as their own adult relationship continues to grow, develop, and thrive. Single parents, who may or may not want to be in a new adult relationship, will also grow and develop especially if they can count on others for support. I'm reminded here of the book *Operating Instructions*, where, as a single parent, Anne Lamott (1993) chronicles her experience raising her son with the support of her dearest friend.

The point of all of this is that parents are not only the primary care-givers of their baby but are also the primary regulators of their infant's physiology. This means that parents need the kind of support that best scaffolds them to do this important work. Since pregnancy and the newborn period, in particular, can be stressful, and stress affects emotional regulation, it's important to give some thought to the kind of support you need. Jay Belsky (1984) put forth a three-point model to determine parenting quality. Here's what it included:

1. The parents' own psychological resources (I would say the parents' own emotional regulation history)

2. The child's unique characteristics (child's temperament)

3. The parents' social support system and stress levels

After reviewing the child-abuse literature, Belsky concluded that the quality of a couple's marital relationship, their social support system, and decisions related to work and income are the three areas most involved with parental competency.

WORK ABSORPTION: BALANCING HOME AND WORK

Work absorption is a term used to describe the parenting characteristics of parents holding professional jobs. One study found that the more intensively involved a father was with his occupation, the more likely he was to be impatient and irritable with his children (Belsky 1984). Since 62 percent of two-parent homes in the United States now have both parents working, work absorption can also be a problem for women. I have personally seen work absorption in a number of mothers. The obvious risk of work absorption is a parent's inability to make mental transitions from work to the baby's world for sensitive communication and attunement. Here's a look at two fathers with professional careers, followed by a look at two mothers with professional careers.

Fathers Transitioning from Work to Home: Hiram and Grant

Hiram and Elizabeth were married with four children, two under five. Hiram told me he couldn't wait to get home to see his wife and kids. He felt like he had an automatic work shut-off valve that went off for him when he left the office, and by the time he walked in the door at home, he felt relief and delight to be with his family.

Grant and Jeanine had one child together and a child from a previous marriage. Grant typically walked into his home thinking about the day and what he had to do tomorrow. He felt tense when he entered his home and didn't like the kids or Jeanine to immediately approach him or interact with him. He needed some transition time before he could join the ongoing lives of his wife and children.

Mothers Transitioning from Work to Home: Annette and Kathryn

Remember Annette and Howard Hatch? Annette worked at home on many nights, but she found it restful and emotionally regulating to be with her children before they went to bed (and before she began working again). She told me it was like "taking a break" to be in her children's world, and it was deeply satisfying to her.

Kathryn and Julian had one fourteen-month-old child. Julian worked from home and provided much of the baby's daily care; a housekeeper helped with the baby when Julian had to go out. When Kathryn came home, she liked to talk to her husband about her day at work before she reoriented to her child. She often struggled with these feelings when she saw how happy the baby was to see her. So Kathryn developed an interesting transition time for herself that included sitting on the sofa with her husband and talking with him with the baby present. Even though she said that she would really like more alone time with her husband when coming in from work, she added, "I'm adjusting, as I can see how important it is for the baby."

Elizabeth and Jeanine, both stay-at-home mothers, had equally complex days living within the world of children. Many stay-at-home mothers and fathers have difficulty finding one hour a day for adult-related activities, like going to the gym, having coffee with a friend, or reading a book. These are real issues that parents face when children come into the world. This is where other family members, such as grandparents, aunts, and uncles, who are committed to the development of the child and family can help out.

The issue is finding the right balance so that you can have the emotional regulation to respond with sensitivity to your child. This will vary between individuals and couples, but it's important for you and your partner to at least consider what it might take to feel regulated enough to be attuned to your child. As you approach the birth of your child, it's a good time to assess as best as you can, "Who is there for me/us?"

BUILDING YOUR FAMILY INFRASTRUCTURE: EXPECT CHANGE

Even the best-laid plans may turn out differently from what you expected. That is what happened to all of these first-time pregnant couples who came to me for both prenatal and postnatal consultations.

Neil and Ann Warren

Neil and Ann were married for several years before they became pregnant. At the prenatal consultation, Neil and Ann stated they were comfortable and happy in their relationship, and I could see that they enjoyed each other's company. Both were employed and said they enjoyed their work. Ann planned to return to work after a three-month pregnancy leave; Neil planned to take some paternity leave to "help out." Both wanted to have a child and were delighted to become pregnant; Neil attended all prenatal visits and classes.

At the postnatal visit, Neil and Ann came in with their adorable four-week-old daughter, Leila. Neil said that he missed Leila during the day and found himself coming home from work earlier than usual. Ann said she couldn't wait to get back to work because the baby was "constantly needing something," and "I can't even take a shower or run an errand anymore." Both of their families were helping the couple so that they could have some breaks. Ann did not report depression.

In this family, Neil was actively engaged in Leila's care and was not just helping out but was also functioning as a primary caregiver. Even so, Ann still needed a break from the baby. In the newborn period, it's common for mothers to need to get out into the adult world a bit, whether with the baby or not. This is where grandparents, friends, or other relatives can help to give the family a break. For Ann, however, these feelings were more intense than is typical, and she actually became closer to Leila after she returned to work. Luckily, Neil was intensely involved in Leila's care, and Neil and Ann continued to be as attuned to each other as they had been in their prior-to-baby relationship. For Leila, the less-intense involvement of her mother appeared to be somewhat mediated through Neil's care.

Jeff and Gretchen Pritchard

Jeff and Gretchen got married during Gretchen's pregnancy. They had struggled as a couple for a number of years and were not expecting to become pregnant when they did. Jeff was happy about the pregnancy; Gretchen was less sure. Jeff attended one prenatal visit and a few prenatal classes. At the prenatal visit in my office, Gretchen said she planned to stay at home after the baby was born; Jeff would be supporting the family financially. At the postnatal visit, Jeff came in holding his handsome six-week-old son, Carl; he talked about how he liked taking his son to work with him. He also said that he understood what his son was communicating better than his wife did. Gretchen looked depressed and told me that her husband didn't mean to be so critical, that "he is just used to saying what he thinks." At one point, she reached for Carl and held him for the remainder of the visit.

The couple's marital conflict was clearly having a negative effect on Gretchen. In addition to experiencing postpartum depression, she felt bad about herself, while expressing an unhealthy belief that her feelings didn't matter. The couple had minimal family support.

Jeff and Gretchen's premarital conflicts thus continued to interfere with their relationship and now were being projected into Carl's developmental world. Jeff appeared to be claiming Carl as his child, while implying that Gretchen was an incompetent mother. As a result, Gretchen felt more and more demoralized. Both were turning to the child to regulate their own hurts and disappointments in each other. Jeff may have been trying to make up for an unhappy marriage by bonding with Carl so exclusively. Conversely, Gretchen might also begin to turn her mind more toward the baby in a more permanent way as a substitute for her unsatisfying marriage. Jeff and Gretchen's style of interacting would not be healthy for any member of the family, particularly Carl. Without therapeutic intervention, Carl would be interacting with unhappy parents whose negative emotions with each other could be felt by him. In fact, the environments created by unhappy parents are usually fraught with sudden bursts of negative feelings that may be frightening and confusing to a child as the parents struggle with their relationship.

Saul and Arlene Armstrong

Saul and Arlene had been married for a year. At the prenatal visit, both described a happy marriage, which included adult children whom Saul had from a previous marriage. Both Saul and Arlene had careers, and Arlene planned to go back to work after her pregnancy leave. Although they'd been planning to start trying to get pregnant the following year, they were very excited about the pregnancy. Saul attended all prenatal visits and classes. At the postnatal visit, Arlene was holding their beautiful five-week-old daughter, Riba. Within seconds, I could see that Arlene was head over heels in love with this baby, and Saul felt proud. Saul easily handled the fact that Arlene was bonkers over Riba. At one point, Saul picked up Riba and successfully burped her. Arlene smiled approvingly and said to the baby, "Your dad's good at this!" When I asked Arlene if she was sad to be returning to work, she said matter-of-factly while looking at the baby, "Oh, I changed my mind on that." She now wanted to stay at home for at least Riba's first year and said she would reevaluate returning to work at that time. They had found a financial solution that would allow Arlene to stay at home. Saul and Arlene also have family support but said, "We want to try to do it on our own."

Saul and Arlene were communicating well with each other, and it was very easy to see the prior-to-baby relationship functioning well and increasing in intimacy. With his previous experience raising his older children, Saul seemed to add an element of stability to Arlene's transition into motherhood. There was no depression in Arlene. In fact, both Saul and Arlene were happy and responsive to the baby. Riba was surrounded by positive feelings, reflecting her parents' overall happiness and playfulness.

Working for Money or for Regulation: Important Decisions

Figuring out work is a big deal. As you can see, work decisions can involve much more than financial considerations. Ann Warren became a better parent when she returned to work. Ann needed work to help regulate herself. With some support and understanding of Leila's way of communicating, Ann was able to be warmer and more responsive to Leila over time. For the Pritchard family, marital counseling and treatment of Gretchen's depression continued well into Carl's first year. Gretchen learned to be more assertive and actually enrolled in a child development class with the goal of opening her own home child care business. Having a future goal where she could have more financial independence and still take care of Carl greatly improved her sense of well-being. It gave her greater emotional regulation. Interestingly, the more assertive Gretchen became, the more she pushed back on Jeff's comments, which began to change the couple's dynamic. Lastly, the Armstrong parents were just in love with life, with each other, and with Riba. In Arlene's case, I believe that returning to work would have severely disrupted her own emotional regulation. The Armstrongs could manage with Saul's financial support. Other families, of course, may not have this choice. I will talk more about working parents in early childhood in chapter 13.

As the above stories illustrate, the nature of your relationship, your social support network, and your work decisions are all important matters, for all three domains can affect your ability to provide sensitive attunement to your child. You will recall Belsky's (1984) three-point model for determining parenting competence: your own psychological resources or emotional regulation history, your child's temperament, and your social support system and stress levels. He found that even when one of these three components is missing, a parent is still likely to be competent. It's when two out of three are stressful that the family system may be compromised and negatively affect the quality of attunement to the baby. Certainly, if all three areas are compromised, babies are at risk. So, no matter who is in the home, commitments need to be made to establish a healthy infrastructure to support you in preparation for birth.

PREGNANCY

Subtle psychological changes in pregnancy prepare parents, particularly the mother, to bond or attach with the newborn. Like entering the locks in the Panama Canal, each trimester has its own psychological elements associated with attachment. Along with obstetric appointments and ultrasounds, the psychological infrastructure for parenthood is developing. In the first trimester, a woman may not look pregnant and may need to remind herself cognitively that she is pregnant, especially if she has very little body feedback. A peculiar kind of mental and physical juggling begins to occur as a future mother continues to go on with her known life while beginning to feel changes in her body and mind. This "capturing of her mind" or her thoughts, as she begins to turn slightly inward, is actually the beginning of a bond she is forming with her yet unborn child. Of course, morning sickness may initially keep her so preoccupied that she will be unaware of these subtleties and may feel quite startled to pass by the full-length mirror one day and exclaim, "What happened here?"

There are multiple elements thought to be involved in a woman's transition to motherhood and the formation of her attachment bond to her newborn. Briefly, some of the factors are as follows: developing a sense of fetal characteristics and intention, differentiating the fetus from yourself, developing interactions with the fetus, giving of yourself, developing a maternal role, feeling anticipation and curiosity about the fetus, imaging yourself as a parent, recognizing the fetus as a person, developing fears, affection, and concerns, and having fantasies about the fetus (Cranley 1981; Muller 1993; Rees 1980).

In a more recent review of studies, Shieh, Kravitz, and Wang (2001) found that three domains appear to be involved with the transition to parenthood:

1.   Parents begin to fantasize about the characteristics of their unborn child.

2. Parents begin to have affection for their unborn child and begin to take pleasure in thinking about their unborn child.

3. Parents take active steps to protect their unborn child and make preparations for the newborn's arrival.

Of course, assessing elements involved in fetal attachment varies greatly by culture, and there is now research assessing a future father's fetal attachment (Pretorius et al. 2006). But generally, cognitive or left-brain feedback commonly experienced in the first trimester dramatically gives way to a new body experience when the baby moves. And, of course, the right brain begins to light up to the new tactile sensations.

FETAL MOVEMENT

Quickening or fetal movement in the second trimester (at about eighteen to twenty weeks' gestation) is a part of a future mother's intersubjective experience and proof that there is a baby in there. Fetal movement also pushes a future mother from the mental idea of having a baby to the concrete reality of "I'm having a baby!" Friends and relatives may hear about the baby moving, and a woman's husband/partner more often than others may get to see and feel the baby move, but the future mother is the only one who is actually experiencing the ongoing tactile/kinesthetic sensations of fetal movement within her own body. And this rhythm carries information for many women.

In this phase, women begin talking to their babies and help the future father understand what the baby is doing. Many future fathers also talk with their babies, but it is the ongoing experience of movement that seems to begin a pattern in a future mother's brain (and that would be her right brain) of what her baby is like. She begins to learn that when she eats a particular food, her baby moves differently. If she startles, her baby responds with a kick. Or when she reads her book with Mozart in the background, she notices that this seems to affect the baby's movement. A sketchy blueprint about who the baby is begins to form in her mind through her felt experience of the baby, even sight unseen. Moving from the external everyday world of events to these interior sensations created by a moving fetus is perhaps one way that nature begins to prepare the future mom for tuning in to her baby. This is, of course, the beginning of a felt relationship to her unborn child, who is quite literally growing within her mother's biological rhythms, hearing sounds of her heartbeat, and experiencing the waves of her hormone cascades.

Circadian rhythms are internal biological rhythms that control the activity of various hormones and neurotransmitters, body temperature, and the sleep-wake cycle. You might have heard these rhythms referred to as your "biological clock." Living systems have circadian rhythms that are generally entrained to the light-dark cycle of the earth. There is evidence that the circadian rhythms of the fetus are present by thirty weeks of gestation but that the fetus nevertheless responds to the mother's circadian rhythms, which are entrained to the light-dark cycle already (Mirmiran et al. 1992). The mother's own circadian rhythms appear to begin to entrain the emerging biological rhythms of her unborn child. Even though a fetus is carrying the genetics from both parents, it is developing within the internal biological rhythms of the mother. This may be why young babies when distressed tend to want their mothers over their equally bonded fathers. They may be seeking a reset or resynchronization of rhythms established in the womb.

By the third trimester, the soon-to-be parents are actively preparing for the arrival of their child. There are baby showers for the parents, as it is becoming increasingly popular to include a future father in this ritual. The fetus can also hear in the third trimester, and it is postulated that this is why babies can recognize their mother's voice at birth (DeCasper and Fifer 1980; Fifer and Moon 1995). Future mothers in their third trimester may begin having some birth anxiety, which seems to give way to a more urgent readiness to "get this baby out" as the due date approaches. But the date does come and labor begins.

APPROACHING THE BIRTH

You both have attended all your birthing classes, learned how to breathe during labor, have done your exercises, the future dad has practiced coaching, and now the suitcase is packed. There will be many details associated with your unique family and circumstances in preparation for the birth. There are a few important decisions, however, that are appropriate for all. The first one for the future mother is whom do you want with you during the birth? Your husband or partner, a close friend, or another family member? Whom do you want in the labor and delivery room with you? And whom would you want close by in the waiting room? It's good to spend some time thinking about what would provide you with the most security while you give birth. If you want others there, it's important to make some arrangements, so this can happen. Sometimes family members and friends can get a bit antsy and may do better in the waiting room, but it may feel comforting to know that they are out there, at least at the beginning of labor. As you will have learned in your child-birth classes, early labor still gives you time to do other things. A friend of mine wanted to play cards while she was in early labor; some women like to walk around. As labor progresses into active labor, however, your attention will be more focused on the immediate moment, and you won't be thinking of much else.

Reduced stress and increased feelings of competence during the birth can improve the quality of the first meeting with your baby. Many couples elect to have a doula (pronounced doo-la) with them at the birth to provide emotional scaffolding. Doulas are trained to provide continuous support during labor and birth. They have attended many a birth and give reassurance to both mother and father without interfering with the labor and delivery doctors and staff. You can interview doulas in your third trimester to find one who feels right for you. In multiple studies, mothers with doula-supported births report less painful births, shorter labors, fewer cesarean deliveries, less anxiety, more positive feelings, decreased depression, and a greater tendency to breastfeed afterwards (Scott, Klaus, and Klaus 1999). Doulas often can help normalize the birthing process for fathers or partners who are experiencing the sights and sounds of labor for the first time. Postpartum doulas can also be helpful to the new family during the newborn period.

For most new mothers and fathers, the hospital stay is only one or two nights, so the second decision to think about prior to birth is who can help out during the newborn period. The newborn period is an intense period that requires ongoing care of the infant while the mother heals and the family begins to adjust to new sleep patterns. It is generally helpful when close family members can do the laundry, cook meals, or do a bit of cleanup for the new family. Throughout my years of clinical practice, however, I have heard a few stories from couples who first wanted to be alone together before interacting much with family and friends; others really appreciated having their immediate family, particularly the mother's mother, around during this period. Before the baby is born, it's also a good idea to consider whether the new dad will take family leave; you can always change your minds about this later.

THE NEW OCEAN: AFTER YOUR BABY IS BORN

It all happens remarkably fast once you look back on it! You've gone through the stages of pregnancy together, crossed an ocean, and now you are on the other side, together with your newborn child. Holding your newborn is not only important for the baby; it is incredibly important for your bonding with her. Most hospitals now put the newborn directly onto the mother or give the baby to the father to hold within minutes of birth. Very soon after birth, parents begin gazing at their newborn, particularly the mother, who is perhaps privately updating her pregnancy sketches with this new live version. Counting fingers and toes and looking at every square inch of the newborn can be immensely pleasurable. Some mothers report an immediate elation upon seeing their baby after the birth and feel deeply bonded; some fathers are so awestruck with seeing their baby born that they feel instantly bonded and incredibly protective of both their wife and baby. New parents often feel a new level of responsibility, maturity, protection, accomplishment, and joy. Sometimes it may take a week or two to feel this, as for some new parents, the bonding proceeds in a slower but incremental fashion with increasing exposure to their baby. It is when there is a prolonged lack of feeling for the baby that other issues may seep in, like postpartum depression and/or personality factors that often require professional help.

Baby Blues vs. Postpartum Depression

It is normal for new mothers to feel the baby blues. In fact, about 25 to 75 percent of new mothers experience the baby blues within three to four days after the birth (Miller and Rukstalis 1999). This is generally thought to be due to the rapid change in a mother's hormones after the birth of a child, and the feelings will remit in a few days without professional help. *Postpartum depression*, however, is a more serious condition that in most cases requires professional assistance. Postpartum depression affects up to 15 percent of women within four weeks of birth (O'Hara 1997). An ongoing lack of enjoyment, increased anxiety and/or sadness, worry and guilt, and an overall feeling of being overwhelmed that won't let up can all be signs of postpartum depression. Immediate intervention is critical if you feel that life is not worth living and/or are having any thoughts of harming yourself or your baby.

Women who have had previous episodes of depression are at greater risk for postpartum depression. Support from spouse/partner, family, and friends, however, is associated with reduced likelihood of postpartum depression (O'Hara 1997). The effects of untreated depression can now affect the baby (as well as the husband/partner), whose eyes find her mother's flat, expressionless, crying face instead of the animated imitation of baby expressions that begins to organize the baby's attachment experience. Certainly the most dangerous condition is postpartum psychosis, which is a depression so severe that a woman loses touch with reality. Postpartum psychosis is rarer than postpartum depression, occurring in one to two births per one thousand; however, it carries more lethal risks to both mother and child because of disorganized thought and homicidal/suicidal ideation (Attia, Downey, and Oberman 1999). For most new families, though, Mom, Dad, and newborn will leave the hospital or birthing center tired but with moods intact.

Breastfeeding

You will have heard about the importance of breastfeeding during your prenatal classes. There is a public campaign encouraging mothers to breastfeed because of its benefits to infants. Breast milk is a complete newborn diet for about six months. It is loaded with enzymes that boost the baby's immune system and help with digestion. In fact, the American Academy of Pediatrics (2005) recommends exclusive breastfeeding for a minimum of six months for optimal infant health benefits, and it encourages mothers to breastfeed for as long as is comfortable for mother and child. Breastfeeding includes some benefits for mothers, as well. Breastfeeding is associated with greater weight loss in the mother who breastfeeds from three to six months postpartum (Dewey 2004). An increase in the hormone prolactin involved in milk production has also been associated with reduced levels of anxiety in the mother (Asher et al. 1995).

Breastfeeding is also wonderful for the newborn's attachment-in-the-making. Feeding your baby through your own body can create calm, satisfying feelings in you, which, in turn, creates lovely ambient feelings for the baby. Furthermore, the newborn is on your body, which helps the baby regulate her biological rhythms. Breastfeeding also feels secure for most babies, and it gives much cozy tactile experience, which is good for your newborn's brain. Remember that the internal working models of attachment start with felt experiences, and warm, cozy, intimate experiences start attachment off on the right track. Fathers can also bottle-feed and hold their infants, fostering their own intimate experiences with their newborn.

THE NEWBORN PERIOD

The newborn period technically begins with the birth of the baby and extends from six to eight weeks after the birth. This is a particularly important time for all concerned. Leaving the hospital is like going through those last canal locks, all of a sudden releasing you into that other big ocean to navigate your new life together. A newborn needs a lot of body contact with her parents as she adjusts to being out of the womb. Generally, a newborn is either on one of your bodies or never further than a few feet away, making it easier to monitor her needs. The immediacy of newborns usually keeps parents in their right brains, as they are learning what newborn cries mean, talking with their newborns, watching their reactions, listening for newborn sounds, and adjusting to newborn characteristics, all while trying to get some sleep themselves!

Newborns are social creatures who arrive prepared to interact. They love human faces, and when they are alert, even a 48- to 72-hour-old newborn can lock onto the eyes of her parents, if held face-to-face about twelve to fifteen inches away, for at least a few seconds (Brazelton 1992; Lundqvist and Sabel 2000). They also like the sound of your voice. Even though newborns are sleeping from fifteen to seventeen hours a day, when they are awake and not hungry, you may find your baby looking at you. If you meet her look with your own expressive face and let your feelings flow, you may have the sense that your baby is smiling at you even though she won't be able to curve her mouth into a smile yet.

Melody and Her Grandmother

Melody was a beautiful, serene two-day-old baby, wrapped in a warm yellow blanket and lying slightly propped up on her parents' bed. Melody looked intensely at her grandmother, who was smiling at her. Melody appeared to have a flush of feeling that registered in changes in her facial tone, which gave her grandmother the feeling that Melody was smiling (something she couldn't do yet). She also opened her mouth a little (a sucking movement that she could do) in response, and her grandmother felt her heart melt. This very intimate communication between Melody and her grandmother amplified their feelings into resonance, and the rest of the world dropped out. This amplification of feeling into resonance has everything to do with bonding and attachment.

KEYS TO ATTACHMENT

Sensitive responding, attunement, resonance, and synchrony all build secure attachments. For the newborn, here are some of the ways you can feel reassured that your attunement is on the secure attachment track; they all support your baby's brain development:

- Hold your baby or have your baby on your body as much as possible; your baby will like your smell and the warm cozy feelings of your body.

- Listen to your baby's communications, so you can learn your baby's unique expressions and characteristics; your baby will like the little space you give her to respond to you.

- Gaze at your baby, face-to-face; make eye contact and respond to your baby's expressions; your baby will love looking at your face and will try to imitate your facial expressions.

- Talk with your baby while you are interacting with her; your baby will love the different intonations and inflections of your voice.

- Respond with sensitivity to your baby's needs; your caring voice and gentle touching while you are feeding, changing, and/or soothing her will indicate to her that you understand she is hungry, needs a diaper change, or is not feeling so good.

- Play with your baby through voicing, tummy rubbing, head stroking, humming, and/or walking with her, so she can take a look around; your baby will begin to be interested in a slightly wider world as she moves through the newborn period.

Attunement during the newborn period is heavily focused on trying to read your newborn's signals and responding to them with sensitivity. Parents begin to learn that their newborn has different cries for different reasons, and this is actually the secret decoder ring for newborn attunement and regulation. Babies can have a hunger cry, a need-a-diaper-change cry, a change-in-position cry, or a fussing-around sound that may mean, "I need a burp," "I need to be held," or "I am sleepy." Babies also have an urgent-alert cry that usually motivates all adults in the vicinity to rapidly advance toward the infant! By observing the response of your newborn, you will begin to figure out what you need to do.

Many important developmental events are occurring within this early period for both the newborn and for you, her parents. The newborn's internal biological clock, for example, is beginning to be entrained to the earth's light-dark cycle, which will eventually lead to greater sleep regulation. Your own sleep cycles are simultaneously desynchronized, however, as you try to respond to your newborn's one- to three-hour feeding schedules. In this period, you will learn about your newborn's unique characteristics, her feeding, sleeping, and interaction needs, all while trying to tend to your own needs, particularly your need for sleep. When a couple is attuned enough to each other, and there is reliable family support and a good pediatrician, a new family will emerge from the newborn period with an infant who is stronger, more interactive, and held by more confident parents.

A Postnatal Visit: Maria and Janice

Maria was a single mother who brought her newborn Janice to my office for their first postnatal visit. A lovely, energetic five-week-old, Janice was dressed in a cute onesie with matching hat and blanket. Maria said that Janice was a fussy baby but used a soft melodic voice while smiling at Janice. Janice responded with a body wiggle and a half-a-lip smile. Janice was intensely watching Maria's face as she talked. Maria said she was breastfeeding and bottle-feeding Janice. Janice fussed a little, and Maria instantly responded to her with a rub on her tummy. In fact, Maria's hand often rested on Janice's tummy. Janice liked the tummy rub for a while, then fussed some more. Maria responded by stopping the rub and offering Janice a bottle that she took, and she began to fall asleep. Janice is a deeply beloved baby, for Maria was unsure she could have a child. She began telling me about how her family had been there for her over the past few weeks, when she looked at Janice and forgot what she was saying (meaning Janice deeply captured her mother's right brain, and I am happy about this).

Maria put Janice at her shoulder and said she was hard to burp. Maria was very gentle with Janice. While she resumed her conversation with me, she shifted Janice to her other shoulder. Janice's head bobbed trying to look at a nearby plant over her mother's shoulder. She then looked up from the plant to the door as if to take in her environment. When I commented to Maria that Janice seemed interested in the plant, Maria said, "Oh, she's very curious. I walk her around our house because she likes to look at things." Fabulous mom! Maria also talked with Janice using different intonations in her voice. The rhythm, tone, and inflection of your voice captivates newborns. Janice was a very regulated baby at five weeks. Maria reported that there had been difficult moments, though, when Janice was colicky. Maria's flexibility, however, was apparent, and she was able to give herself over to responding to her newborn's needs. I could also see that Maria had been discovering Janice's characteristics and knew quite a lot about her newborn, even after only five weeks.

IN A NUTSHELL: TAKE CARE OF YOURSELVES

CHAPTER 4

We're Still Breathing!
The Two-Month-Old

I am your favorite book; you are my new lines.
I am your night-light; you are my starshine.
—Maryann Cusimano, *You Are My I Love You*

By two months, parents generally begin seeing more consistency in their
infant's eating and sleeping routines and feel more confident in their
parenting. Often as they start to feel like they know their infant, parents
begin to feel a sense of pride and accomplishment. For many couples,
the more predictable patterns in their infants begin to trigger moments
of reflection about each other and their new experience that was quite
impossible during the newborn period. When interviewing a couple with
a new baby, I commonly ask how they now see each other. Some of the
most beautiful, sensitive moments occur during these conversations as
each person hears how the other now sees him or her as a mother or
father. Karen, a new mother, felt a surge of love for her husband, George,
as she described a recent experience. She was in the shower and thought
the baby was crying, so she peeked out the bathroom door. Instead of

hearing the baby crying, she heard her husband laughing and talking with the baby. George also felt increasingly proud of Karen as he watched her responding to their baby. These new perceptions of each other as parents can widen and deepen your relationship bond, making it easier for you to respond to your infant's needs with sensitivity and confidence.

SETTING THE SCENE: JORDAN'S NEED FOR CONTACT

"Jordan is eight weeks and one day old," his father Neal proudly announced while looking at his wife, Alice. Alice and Neal were referred by their pediatrician for a postpartum evaluation and were sitting in my office with Jordan, a handsome baby with thick hair combed and parted neatly to one side. Jordan sat in an infant carrier between his parents. His body was somewhat still, and he was leaning toward his mother. Jordan seemed to be staring at his mother. In fact, Jordan stared at his mother for most of the interview until he fell asleep. His mother made glances at him but never held his eyes. Whenever Jordan fussed, either Neal or Alice held a bottle up for him while they continued to talk. He was taken out of the infant seat for a burp by his father and then returned. Two things stood out:

1.   The couple appeared to have an intense need for each other that overrode attunement to their son.

2.   The baby was signaling an intense need for eye contact, especially from his mother.

Although Alice and Neal were taking good care of their baby's physical needs, they were struggling with expressing genuine warmth for or delight over Jordan. I'll return to Jordan, Alice, and Neal later in the chapter, when I discuss cultivating secure attachment in two-month-olds. First, you need to become familiar with the physical, emotional, and brain development in this age group.

DEVELOPMENTAL MILESTONES: BUILDING CONNECTION AS YOUR BABY GROWS

Development of the brain systems is associated with the changes in development that you will naturally see in your child. Your sensitive-enough and attuned interactions with your baby will both support development as well as build your relationship. Understanding how to interact with your baby as he develops within each growth stage is important to support the unique tasks for that stage. But although the tasks of development change, what needs to remain constant enough throughout development is his reliable relationship with you, his parents. It's like a piece of music where the bass line is held constant as the melody progresses. When parents are constant enough in their ongoing, attuned emotional regulation, their child's self-development gets stronger and more confident. Soon the child's very self will begin to write the melody with his own interests while parents help scaffold the cognitive, language, and motor integration needed at each developmental stage. It is really quite elegant. And most parents would likely not think of what they are doing as they go along; they just do it seamlessly. For example, Doneva, a first-time mother, gave a running commentary to her daughter Keesha from the minute she was born. Whether it was changing her diapers, fixing her bottle, dressing her, or putting her in the car seat, she talked with Keesha about what they were experiencing together. Although Doneva was building a wonderfully intimate relationship with Keesha that was full of eye contact, she was also supporting her language development as she talked with her. As it turned out, when Keesha was twelve months old, she coded secure on her developmental assessment and she had the language development of an eighteen- to twenty-four-month-old. This is an example of how parents support the developmental tasks within an ongoing, secure relationship with their child. Such support needs to occur throughout the developmental period and, in some fashion, will continue throughout life, as parents support the accomplishments of their children, no matter how old they are. With that said, here's a look at what two-month-olds can do.

Your Baby's Physical and Emotional Development

Although nature has wide ranges for typical development, in general, the two-month-old begins to do the following:

- Hold his head more erect and steady

- Try to elevate himself with his arms when placed on his stomach

- Roll from side to back or back to side

- Anticipate feeding with a sucking movement

- Smile responsively to your smile

- Rhythmically kick or make bicycle movements when excited

- Brighten his eyes, seek your eyes, and coo and gurgle to communicate

- Focus on faces and objects from eight to ten feet away

- Move his eyes to follow you as you move

- Turn his head and eyes toward interesting sounds

- Imitate exaggerated faces

- Turn away from eye contact if he needs a rest from stimulation

- Express his emotions using total body movements

Your Baby's Brain Development

At birth, the newborn's amygdala is modulating physical arousal while other systems are activated depending upon the infant's experience. As discussed in chapter 2, the amygdala is a primitive regulatory system that is fully operating at birth (Schore 2001a), and it is capable of activating the SNS and the PNS as needed to keep the baby's autonomic nervous system in balance. There are ranges of activation, of course, but as a reminder, the SNS can be seen when the infant is crying or is in an excited state while PNS activation can be seen when an infant is relaxed or sleepy. Primary caregivers begin to regulate their baby's interior world of physiology through holding, eye contact, sounds, facial expressions, and sensitive responding to their infant's needs.

Close infant-caregiver contact not only regulates the baby's temperature but also puts the infant within eye contact range of the mother. Mother-infant eye gazing activates both the mother's and infant's right hemisphere, especially if the infant is held on the mother's left side. Positive mutual gazing experiences begin to establish an intimate, nonverbal synchrony between mother and infant, providing the foundation for secure attachment. Positive gazing and voicing also stimulate pleasurable feelings in the infant, which, in turn, releases neurochemicals needed for the growth of dendrites in the visual and auditory cortices, which are in a sensitive growth period at this age (de Graaf-Peters and Hadders-Algra 2006). So again, you see that while you are building your secure relationship with your baby, his brain states are developing at the same time. The visual, auditory, and tactile sensations that your baby experiences through you are directly supporting the neuronal growth and development in parts of the brain known as the occipital, temporal, and parietal lobes, which are specialized for visual, auditory, and tactile information, respectively (see figure 1 in chapter 2).

New Skills

- He likes interesting sounds and will turn his head and eyes in the direction of the sound.

- He prefers human voices and will often make vowel vocalizations in response.

- He often smiles when spoken to and will try to imitate exaggerated facial expressions.

- He can briefly hold on to a finger or a toy if placed in his hand.

- He likes to look at patterns, particularly high contrast black-and-white patterns. He also likes to follow the movement of a brightly colored mobile.

- His eyes will follow you, and you might find him looking at other objects in his environment, especially if he is sitting up or at your shoulder. He will study faces, particularly the faces of his primary caregivers. He loves eye contact, particularly when it is paired with interesting changes in your voice.

- He has smoother motor movements than he did at one month, and he can often show increased rhythmic body movements when excited.

- He is now practiced at feeding and will often anticipate feeding at the sight of the breast or bottle.

- He will startle to a loud noise and will need to be soothed, but he is also beginning to use self-soothing behaviors like sucking on a hand or pacifier.

- The two-month-old can signal when he wants to interact by brightening his eyes, cooing, seeking eye contact, and smiling. He can also signal when he needs to disengage by frowning, breaking eye contact, and/or turning his head away.

CULTIVATING SECURE ATTACHMENT IN THE TWO-MONTH-OLD

Again, studies on parental attunement show that most parents are attuned about a third of the time, with the rest of the time spent in misattunement and repair. Also recall that 100 percent perfect attunement creates very narrow arousal ranges, which can limit the child's coping ability, while chronic misattunement without repair will create a dysregulated nervous system. As you can see, it's neither realistic nor desirable to be completely attuned to your baby all the time, but you can do tremendous good for your child by learning to attune to him. Parents who play with their infant are increasing the child's positive affect, and parents who respond to their infant's crying states with sensitivity are decreasing negative affect. Increasing positive while regulating negative affect is what entrains optimal arousal ranges in your baby's nervous system. When a parent is able to be a good enough regulator of the infant's arousal, his body feels good to him, especially when there are more feel-good feelings than feel-bad feelings, thereby freeing him to experience and learn about his world within the safety of his parent's protection. This all will lead to his ability to regulate his own emotions as he feels secure enough to learn and explore.

Jordan, Alice, and Neal: Strengthening Emotional Connection

So now, think again about two-month-old Jordan and his parents, Alice and Neal. Remember that as Jordan stared at his mother, she didn't return his gaze. There was also very little holding, touching, and cuddling, as Jordan was often fed by bottle propping. Jordan was deprived of all the rich experiences that would be provided through intimate, attuned interactions with his mother. Without a doubt, his parents loved him and were providing for his basic physical care with some sensitivity, yet Jordan was telling me through his staring that it wasn't enough; he needed more attunement, more holding and cuddling, and definitely more positive face-to-face interaction. He needed Alice's internal feeling world.

This was hard for Alice, who'd had a difficult upbringing herself. She described her mother as "incompetent" and "a waste of time." She said, "She never seemed to get me." Also, Alice had not been sure she wanted a baby but had agreed to it because her husband wanted to have a family. By caring for Jordan's physical needs in a timely fashion, Alice was trying to raise her son better than she'd been raised. However, where she ran into her own working model of attachment was when she needed to respond to her son's nonverbal, intimate need of her internal feeling world. This was where Alice had difficult feelings about giving and mothering.

With encouragement, Alice felt secure enough to acknowledge that she knew the baby was staring at her and needed her attention. I asked Alice to come to a few sessions with Jordan and encouraged her to put him on a blanket on the sofa next to her. Perhaps because she didn't want Jordan to roll off the sofa, she would put her hand on Jordan's chest. (This was her left hand by the way, which is controlled by her right hemisphere.) As we talked about her life and how she wanted to be a better mother than her mother, I noticed that she would gently rub Jordan's chest almost unconsciously. This was a very good sign that Alice's feelings for Jordan were beginning to be more intimate. Rubbing his chest often prompted a coo from Jordan, which led to Alice's looking at Jordan and smiling at him. Jordan began responding with smiles, which gave Alice a feeling that her baby also responded to her. Alice began to feel more confident in their relationship and better about herself, which gave her more room to express her feelings of love for Jordan.

When they left treatment, Alice's expressive face-to-face eye contact had increased dramatically. Jordan responded with increased excited leg and body kicking, cooing, babbling, and smiling. Alice also learned that she needed time to herself for her own emotional regulation. She and Neal worked out a plan together, allowing Alice to set some boundaries, which would support the formation of their new family.

GAMES: Smiles and Sounds

- Two-month-old babies love eye contact and expressive, exaggerated faces. A fun baby game can be lifting your eyebrows, widening your eyes, and watching your baby study you or imitate you. Playing around with different sounds like clicking your tongue is very interesting to your baby, but loud voices or sounds can startle him.

- Singing a lullaby to your baby while rocking him or singing a song while bathing him can be fun for both of you. If you associate a particular song to an activity, your baby will begin to expect the activity as soon as he hears the song. This is particularly helpful when putting him down for sleep.

- Different sounds, like soft chimes or a rattle, may interest your baby.

- Stroking his hair, rubbing his tummy, or gently walking your fingers from tummy to neck while saying "I see you" is also fun for your baby.

- Walking with the baby at your shoulder allows him to see different views. This also gives him a chance to strengthen his neck muscles, even though you are still providing head support. Interesting pictures on the wall or the sight of a plant may capture your baby's interest, at least for a few moments.

- If you see your baby studying something, saying to him that "you really are interested in that" will help both of you to register what your baby likes.

- Reading an infant book to your baby will visually stimulate him, and the sound of your voice is comforting to him. You can talk with him about what you see in the book. He also sees you turning pages, which is interesting for him. Before you know it, he will grab the book and turn the pages himself.

- Two-month-olds love patterns. Your baby probably enjoys tracking objects, like a good-looking rattle, which you can hold up for him and move back and forth so that he can follow it with his eyes. Having interesting mobiles within visual range will also entertain him. These toys can provide learning experiences within the intimacy of your relationship.

95

PLAY AND ATTACHMENT IN THE TWO-MONTH-OLD

When you play with your baby, he plays back through his cooing, focused or wide eyes, kicking legs, brightening face, raised eyebrows, smiles, and vocalizations. He can purse his lips into an "O," making an "oooh" sound, perhaps followed by tongue clicking. Doing all this, the baby is intensively interacting with his caregiver, and it's a sign of positive play at this age. You will begin to learn what your baby likes as you watch his facial expressions, body movements, and vocalizations. Your baby signals negative emotions as clearly as positive ones, and you can learn to recognize these too. When your baby needs to disengage, he might turn his head away, lower his eyes, or show a frown. By verbalizing his feelings for him, saying "you're tired of this now" or "you didn't like that," you show your baby that you understand him and will respond sensitively to his needs. You will also begin to understand what he likes and doesn't like. This is attunement. Reading your baby's internal, nonverbal state and responding to him with sensitivity gives your baby a feeling of security.

PARENT FOCUS: REENTERING THE ADULT WORLD

Rhonda had not been out much since the birth of her three-month-old but decided to accept an invitation to a party at her yoga studio. She arrived with Erin, who was bundled up in an infant pouch on her mother's chest, and her older daughter, Carmen. I noticed that when Rhonda was talking to her friends, she stroked Erin's head. Rhonda had that wonderful ability to do left- and right-brain communication simultaneously. She was clearly enjoying her friends' attention to her and the baby.

Meanwhile, three-year-old Carmen was dancing around in her socks nearby. Rhonda smiled at Carmen and decided to sit down on the floor next to the wall. As Rhonda sat down, she put Erin in the crook of her arm, facing out, so Erin could watch what was going on, while Carmen climbed up on Rhonda's other side. Rhonda's friend also came and sat with her on the floor. Rhonda sat talking with her friend while Erin practiced her eye tracking. Although her eyes were not quite smooth in their tracking yet, she followed one set of legs and then another as they crossed the floor at her eye level. Rhonda saw this and commented, "You like the people moving, don't you?" What an incredibly competent mom, to be able to enjoy herself with her friends while continuing to attune to both of her children. The intimacy around this family was thick, sustaining, and real.

LIVING IN THE CHARM: PIPPA'S RESPONSE TO HER NEW THREE-MONTH-OLD COUSIN

Living with young children is not all bustle; it's a special time that passes all too quickly. Over the years, many an adorable story has come my way from parents about their children. At the end of each of these developmental chapters, I'd like to pass along one of these stories about children age birth to five. This will help to close each chapter on a light note.

My friend Maggie from my writing group had a new grandbaby named Ingo, who had been absorbing much of the family's attention, from grandparents on down. Recently, Maggie was babysitting another grandchild, Ingo's cousin Pippa, a precocious three-year-old girl. While reading a book on animals, Maggie asked Pippa if she had any pets. Pippa paused, thought carefully, and said, "I have two dogs ... a lot of fish," and pausing again, added, "and an Ingo."

CHAPTER 5

There *Is* Someone in There!

The Four-Month-Old

One Sunday morning the warm sun came up and—pop!—out of the egg came a tiny and very hungry caterpillar.
—Eric Carle, *The Very Hungry Caterpillar*

When a four-month-old looks at you, you can feel and see that she's in there. In fact, the four-month-old will not be shy about looking at you with a slow and steady gaze, leaving you with the impression that she is studying you. On the train to Los Angeles a few weeks back, I was reading when I had the sensation that someone was looking at me. A four-month-old boy, who'd been sleeping in his mother's arms, had awakened and begun studying me. I smiled. He smiled back and then fell asleep again. His security was palpable as he turned toward his mother, who was gently running her fingers over his cheek, and snuggled in.

By this age, everyone is generally sleeping better, and parents are more comfortable with their baby's care. Four-month-olds are much more interactive and easily smile and coo to express themselves. Parents begin feeling captured by their baby's expressions and are regularly engaged in magical moments of interaction. For most parents, by four months, the attachment bond is solidified, unconditional, and absolute. If this is your first time having a child, you may feel changes in your relationship as a couple, now that you have successfully managed the newborn period and are resting upon your lived-together experience. You may notice a greater confidence in each other. Parents may have moments of reflection at this stage or may pause to feel how different their lives are now. These are normal and important psychological changes, integrating the old with the new. This transition is generally assisted, however, by the love for your baby, whose smile and coo makes you wonder, "How could I have ever lived without her?"

At this stage, new parents begin to notice that more has occurred than the birth of their child. A second, more psychological birth has been forming and solidifying through your experiences together in the care of your baby. Around this time, when there is a bit more rest, you might consciously experience the beauty of this other birth ... the birth of your family. This realization can help parents feel a new sense of confidence and security with themselves, thereby giving them more emotional fuel to respond with sensitivity to their baby.

SETTING THE SCENE: CHINA'S NEED FOR PREDICTABLE INTERACTIONS

China was a cute four-month-old girl, but one with a knitted brow, unfocused eyes, and her hands clasped together when she came in with her mother and father to talk with me. The couple had been referred for a postpartum evaluation by their pastor, as the pastor felt that China was "unhappy." China appeared tense and she made no vocalizations during the interview. She was sitting on her mother Erika's knee while Erika talked with me. Her father, Morris, sat quietly beside Erika and did not interact with China. During the interview, it became clear that Morris, who had three other children from a previous marriage, was having difficulty being a father for the fourth time. Although he initially wanted to have a baby with Erika, he became disengaged from Erika after China was born. In fact, Erika stated that she could feel him pulling away emotionally when they were in the delivery room, and by the time they came to me for a consultation, he was sleeping in another bedroom. Erika was doing her best to care for China, but she missed Morris's interaction and felt that she had lost their prior-to-baby relationship. Several issues stood out:

1. The formation of a family unit was compromised in that Morris preferred to remain outside of the newly forming family; Morris also appeared depressed.

2. Erika was beginning to feel grief over the loss of Morris and felt rejected when she tried to move back into her adult relationship with him. She was also feeling overwhelmed with the sole responsibility of China.

3. China appeared to be affected by her parents' conflict, for she did not have the openness or curiosity that is typical of a four-month-old; neither did she smile or vocalize. In fact, she appeared stressed, worried, and emotionally flat.

Although Erika was sensitive to China most of the time, it became clear that her own need for interaction with Morris caused her to become preoccupied with worry. The worry reflected in her face was similar to what could be seen on China's face. I'll return to China, Erika, and Morris when I discuss secure attachment in four-month-olds, but first here's a look at typical physical, social-emotional, and brain development for this age group.

DEVELOPMENTAL MILESTONES: BUILDING CONNECTION AS YOUR BABY GROWS

Again, although the tasks of development change as your baby grows, what needs to remain constant for healthy development and secure attachment is a reliable relationship with attuned enough parents. As would be expected, a baby's developmental tasks involve more complexity as the brain grows and develops. For instance, the three- to four-month-old can visually discriminate differences between two black-and-white patterns and tends to show a preference for the more novel (complex) pattern. Responding to your baby's greater curiosity, interests, and expressions not only supports development; it continues to fuel the brain with needed biochemicals and lays the foundation for secure attachment.

Your Baby's Physical and Social-Emotional Development

In general, the four-month-old can do the following:

- Hold her head erect

- Begin sitting with support

- Begin reaching and grasping small objects, like a teething ring or rattle, and explore it by putting it in her mouth

- Use her hands and eyes in coordination and keep her hands open

- Look toward the source of a sound

- Babble and giggle

- Smile easily

- Inspect her own hands

- Begin to vocalize using consonant-vowel sounds like "da," "ba," "pa"

- Express a range of emotions, like joy, contentment, restlessness, and tiredness

- Use self-soothing behaviors, like sucking her own fingers

Your Baby's Brain Development

The dendritic growth in the temporal and occipital lobes, specialized for the processing of auditory and visual information, reaches a maximum density at about three months (de Graaf-Peters and Hadders-Algra 2006). By four months, you are likely seeing the results from all of your positive face and eye gazing, pleasant voicing, and sensitive responding with your infant, for it has everything to do with your baby's increased abilities. Dynamic proliferations of neurons are organizing into increasingly complex patterns in your baby's brain. *Myelination*, the coating of axons with a fatty substance that allows faster brain transmission of information, is also occurring and will continue throughout the first year of life (de Graaf-Peters and Hadders-Algra 2006). By three months, your infant's stress hormones are assuming their adult circadian patterns, thereby giving your infant better stress modulation, especially if you are doing a good job of regulating her physiology (Gunnar and Donzella 2002). Her sleep rhythm is also assuming an adult pattern, so she is sleeping more during the night (Kennaway, Stamp, and Goble 1992). Beginning at three months and continuing through to nine months, a growth period is occurring in the *anterior* (toward the front) *cingulate gyrus* (see figure 1 in chapter 2), which is associated with laughter, play, exploration, and the onset of increased responsivity to social cues in parent-infant interactions (Schore 2001a). The anterior cingulate is also capable of modulating the autonomic nervous system. When development gets to this level, the infant is moving past the survival gates of the amygdala into a higher regulatory center, based upon the infant's attachment needs being adequately met. As the infant feels safe and secure because her parents are meeting her needs, her development proceeds naturally toward increased complexity, which gives her greater social-emotional capabilities.

New Skills

- She likes to have "conversations" with her primary caregivers. As you talk with her, she likes to look at your eyes and talk back, using smiles, wiggles, gurgles, giggles, and consonant-vowel sounds like "da," "ba," and "pa."

- She recognizes the faces of her primary caregivers.

- She likes to study the faces of new people and will respond to most with a smile if they actively try to speak to her with increased feeling in their voice while holding her eyes. But not too close or too loud as she might startle and turn away.

- She can easily signal when she wants to play and can play for longer periods of time before needing to take a break.

- She has better visual-motor coordination and likes to try reaching for a rattle or a teething ring. She will begin to carry these toys to her mouth for further exploration.

- She can rotate her wrist, thereby making it easier to reach for things.

- She likes to practice sitting for a while, especially if she is supported.

- She can push up on her forearms, when she's placed on her tummy, and try to reach for an interesting toy close by.

- She tries to soothe herself by sucking on her fingers when she is tired, but she still needs her parents' help when she is distressed.

CULTIVATING SECURE ATTACHMENT IN THE FOUR-MONTH-OLD

As you can see, the four-month-old naturally likes increased interaction, as her brain is developing greater complexity. Providing good-enough interactive regulation of her arousal so that she has more positive than negative feelings not only helps your infant to physically feel good but also gives her the vitality to explore, grasp, reach, express herself, and experience her world. It also provides the biochemical fuel she needs for development. Her parents *are* her world at this age (and this won't change significantly for quite a while), but she is beginning to venture out a little as she notices other people and experiences new sights and sounds. So now that you know what a typical four-month-old looks like, here's another look at China, who was not developing typically.

China, Erika, and Morris: Forming a Strong Family Bond

Again, the four-month-old usually has increased vitality, which she expresses in greater interest in others and in exploring a few objects. The four-month-old quite easily smiles at just about anyone who interacts with her with positive affect. It's as if she's popped out of the cocoon of the newborn period into increased baby interactions, as if to say, "Hi, I'm here." Much of this change is because a higher regulatory center in the brain has started to go online. So for China, something was amiss. She lacked vitality and expressiveness, and her body was closed, tense, and still. This meant that China may not have been getting enough positive interaction, which increases vitality and builds the biochemicals needed for healthy brain development.

As it turned out, Erika was much more worried about her relationship with Morris than she was consciously aware of. She felt lonely and scared because she felt solely responsible for China. She didn't feel Morris's interest in her or the baby, which created a real dilemma in forming their secure family bond. Although she was caring for China's physical needs pretty well, she often left China alone for longer periods of time than she realized, because her own emotional regulation was compromised. Erika would also suddenly pick up China at unexpected times to cuddle her for her own comfort. Once, when we were talking about her loneliness, Erika spontaneously picked up sleeping China and began kissing her into an awake state. China was not ready for this attention, so she scrunched up her face and fussed, an interaction that Erika was not looking for. Clearly, what China was learning through her experience with her parents had much to do with unpredictability and confusion, as her mother was mis-attuned much of the time and offered little to no repair. In this case, Erika's needs were more primary than China's emotional needs. Morris's interaction with China was also problematic, as his depression showed on his face. Remember that infants are responding more to nonverbal feeling states, how faces look, and tone of voice than to words or good intentions. China's parents had good intentions, but they were unaware of how their emotional conflict was affecting China.

Through family therapy, with some individual sessions for Morris and Erika, it became clear that Morris had some unresolved issues with his former wife and had not emotionally separated from that marriage because of his children. The previous marriage had been difficult for Morris, and he had complex feelings about leaving his kids, even though he was still active in their lives. Having a new baby with Erika put a strain on this dynamic, leaving Morris with the untenable emotional solution of splitting himself between two women. Morris became conscious of this in therapy and learned that he could emotionally separate from his former wife without emotionally separating from his children. He also learned that he could make an emotional commitment to his new family and include his other children to create a blended family. The underbelly of this emotional conflict was Erika. Being a first-time mom, she'd had the hidden hope that her family would just include the three of them, something Morris, of course, couldn't do. Both were unhappy. Even though Erika and Morris were doing their best to interact with China in a positive way, their unhappiness affected the quality of their attunement.

Over the next several months, the couple began adjusting to the reality of Morris's other children and began making a blended family. They started slowly, with both agreeing that when his children were over, they would do things together. As their new blended family began to take shape, Morris felt more at ease and began interacting more with Erika and China. Erika did a wonderful job of stretching herself to include

Morris's children, which was felt by Morris as including "all" of him as well. The change in China was also remarkable. Erika and Morris began to interact with her together and to follow her cues, which helped all of them to feel more unity. China responded with increased vitality, excited kicking, and greater curiosity as her parents focused more consistent attention on her. Erika began to feel more secure in her relationship with Morris, and they started sleeping together again. When they terminated treatment, China was sitting in her father's lap grasping a rattle and gave me a big smile followed by a gurgle.

PLAY AND ATTACHMENT IN THE FOUR-MONTH-OLD

When you play with your four-month-old, she will play back with vocalizations, smiles, giggles, wiggles, and a happy, excited face. She is able to play now for longer periods of time before needing a break. You are now becoming increasingly familiar with her cues for disengagement, food, diaper change, sleep, and more play. You are probably feeling more like you understand what your baby likes and dislikes. Supporting your child's growing attachment involves continuing to respond sensitively to her needs, including her growing need for more play interactions. You know how long to play with your four-month-old as, using your instincts, you are able to tune in to her internal physiology and can feel when she is getting tired. You also have more experience with your baby and can read her cues more easily; you know that when she turns her eyes or head away from you, she needs a break. Your ongoing, sensitive attunement to her nonverbal, internal state is building her sense of security.

Many new parents begin to feel more like themselves at this stage and feel increasingly confident with baby care. Self-care will continue to be important, especially if parents are returning to work. (I will talk more about child care in chapter 13.) Taking care of your relationship with each other is also important, as your new family relationship becomes more predictable. A night out is a good idea.

GAMES: Reaching and Giggling

- Four-month-olds love interaction and will especially enjoy intimate and expressive face-to-face contact, as you use your eyes and your voice. Even when you talk with your four-month-old from across the kitchen, she will orient to your voice. She also likes seeing "the baby" in the mirror.

- She still loves to be held, rocked, and stroked gently.

- She likes to hear you sing to her, especially a song like "This Little Piggy" which involves physical play. She doesn't mind at all if you sing the song over and over again. She'll also like playing "Patty-cake" with you.

- She likes to look at infant books with you while you read to her and to hear the modulations in your voice. She likes to watch you turn the pages too.

- She loves to giggle when something catches her fancy. If you can figure out what you did and repeat it, both of you will feel immense pleasure.

- Putting your baby on a blanket on the floor on her tummy with a few interesting toys close by will not only support her reaching and exploration but will encourage her to push up on her forearms in preparation for crawling. Some babies don't like to be on their tummies for too long, though, especially if they have just eaten.

- Talking to her about her environment is especially wonderful, and when you repeat back (mirror) what she says, she will know you are listening and that you understand her communications.

- She loves to reach and hold something in her hands and to bring it to her mouth. Soon she will be able to transfer an object from one hand to the other.

PARENT FOCUS: CELEBRATIONS

Ashley and Kevin decided to accept an invitation to a party that another couple was giving to celebrate a birthday. It was a night party and they thought long and hard about leaving their four-month-old, Kayla, with Ashley's parents for the evening, but finally they decided to go. For the first time since late pregnancy, Ashley felt like dressing up, and she went to the party looking terrific. Of course, Kevin responded with interest, and they danced together most of the evening. Both felt relaxed and happy with the chance to have each other in the adult world. For this moment, they felt like the lovers they were, and their intimacy naturally returned.

LIVING IN THE CHARM: DANIEL'S ATTEMPT TO HELP

Twenty-two-month-old Daniel and his family were out to dinner early one evening at a restaurant. Another family was seated nearby, and their four-month-old, Rosa, was sitting in a car seat and not at all happy. She was fussing and crying with her mother, who was trying to soothe her. Daniel, who was standing next to his mother, walked over to the baby, put his hand on the car seat to comfort her, and began singing, "Da eels on da bus go rown and rown."

CHAPTER 6

Knowing the Clan:
The Six-Month-Old

Here's a little baby, one, two, three, sits on his sis-
ter's lap, what does he see? He sees his grandma
ironing, his father pouring tea, his other sister
squabbling, she wants him on her knee.
—Janet and Allan Ahlberg, *Peek-a-Boo!*

The six-month-old knows his clan and is quite comfortable in his daily family life. His comfort with other important people who have been in his world has increased dramatically, and he will interact with grandparents, siblings, and familiar people with a matter-of-fact ease as long as there are not other competing needs, like hunger, fatigue, or not feeling good. For many parents, living with their six-month-old is a stabilizing time, for now both parents and child are used to their established routines. The six-month-old has some familiarity with how the family works and has grown to anticipate many routines, making it easier to make transitions. In fact, routines are critical, as they not only provide some sense of order in the household but also allow your baby to anticipate an event, which is good for his emotional regulation and his thinking skills.

For example, six-month-old Daryl transitioned easily from play to a diaper change because his parents had always talked to him when changing his diaper. In the newborn period, this had been hard as he cried a lot when his diaper was changed. But his parents had talked with him anyway, using a soothing and empathic tone, saying "I know you don't like this, but we have to get you cleaned up." As he got a little older, this turned into a nice tummy tickle and giggle game whenever he was able to tolerate changing, and at six months, all Daryl's parents had to say was "let's get rid of this stinky," and it worked most of the time. They said this, using a playful or warm voice, depending on his mood.

Routines in early childhood help to scaffold everyday life and provide the important supports needed for your six-month-old's ever-increasing curiosity. You are likely now good at reading his nonverbal signals and are feeling less confused about your baby's communications. His skills are exploding, and you might suddenly find that your baby is beginning to be curious about cause-and-effect relationships. This is the age where your baby will actively look on the floor for a spoon that has dropped and might have a perplexed look if one of his expected routines is greatly altered. Your routines and your sensitive emotional regulation of your baby's internal world of feelings continue to be the right recipe for learning, exploration, and secure attachment. When you are holding your baby's interior physiology in a good enough balance, he will not be distracted by uncomfortable internal feelings, and this allows him to naturally learn and explore. All of this is accomplished through your continued attunement and your routines.

SETTING THE SCENE: COREY AND HIS YOUNG MOTHER

Corey was an adorable six-month-old boy who was brought to my office by his mother, Stephanie, at the suggestion of her mother. Stephanie was a young, single mother, raising her baby with support of family and friends. All three of us were sitting on the floor, with Corey on a blanket banging a rattle. He clearly was teething, as he chewed vigorously on his teething ring and drooled but gave a big smile to me while Stephanie wiped his mouth. Stephanie described Corey as a "very good-natured baby," but she was worried of late because he had been clinging, crying, and fussing more. The pediatrician said that Corey was teething and was fussy because of it, but Stephanie thought it was more than that, for he was babbling less, was resisting his bath, and would turn away from her after brief moments of peekaboo that he "used to love." Stephanie began crying at this point and said, "He doesn't seem to want me around now." Two issues stood out:

1. Although Corey was teething, he was still quite interested in exploring and was very sociable.

2. Stephanie was worried and felt rejected by Corey.

It was obvious to me that Stephanie adored her baby. Even though she was young, she had the benefits and experience of a strong family, particularly her mother, and she also had committed friendships. Corey looked like a normal, teething baby with typical fussiness. Stephanie's reaction was more my concern. If prolonged, her own worry and unhappiness might eventually be felt by Corey, who could then react to her differently, thereby setting up and reinforcing a cycle of misattunement. I will return to Corey and Stephanie when I discuss secure attachment in six-month-olds, but first here's a look at typical physical, social-emotional, and brain development for this age group.

DEVELOPMENTAL MILESTONES: BUILDING CONNECTION AS YOUR BABY GROWS

Six-month-olds actively explore, and their nonverbal comprehension has greatly increased. They love all forms of peekaboo games. If you hide something under a cup in front of a six-month-old, he might reach for the cup with both hands and look under it. Your good enough regulation of your baby's emotions is really paying off now as your baby's curiosity is exploding. In fact, you are likely closely tracking your infant's response as his play begins to show his preference for certain toys. Six-month-old David was shown a few toys in his testing evaluation. One was a small rabbit that he reached for. He held it, carried it to his mouth, transferred it to his other hand, banged it, vocalized a couple of "aahs" and "das," and screamed when we tried to substitute a cube for the rabbit. Even though he was eventually able to explore the other toys, every time he saw the rabbit, he reached for it. David showed a preference for this toy. You are likely now quite aware of your baby's preferred objects, games, and routines.

Your Baby's Physical and Social-Emotional Development

In general, the six-month-old can do the following:

- Roll from his back to his tummy

- Sit with support

- Grab his feet and rock around when he's on his back

- Reach, hold, mouth, and bang interesting objects for exploration

- Start to scoot or pull himself toward an object

- Transfer objects from one hand to the other

- Vocalize and babble using the rhythm of language, so it sounds like he's talking … he is!

- Smile when he sees himself in a mirror (he doesn't know it is himself yet)

- Look for objects that disappear or fall off the table

- Recognize his name and look in the direction of your pointing

- Understand your tone of voice

Your Baby's Brain Development

Axons, dendrites, and synapses are continuing to form in your baby's brain, increasing the organization and maturation of the subcortical-to-cortical circuitry. The ongoing maturation and wiring of the anterior cingulate and areas in the parietal lobe are thought to be involved in the infant's expanded abilities at this age, including the ability to anticipate (Schore 2001a). Cortical connections involved in voice and face processing are maturing and integrating. Having the capacity to anticipate greatly expands the infant's ability to understand what certain tones of voice mean. Parental faces, particularly the mother's face, are beginning to serve as highly charged reference points for soothing, play, and emotional regulation.

An infant who has experienced ongoing positive play sequences that are synchronous with his emotions, in addition to sensitive regulation of his negative emotions, will now release the same positive biochemicals just by looking at his parent's face or hearing his parent's voice. The tone and rhythm of language, called *prosody*, is the result of the greater maturation and organization of the brain, particularly the maturing anterior cingulate and right temporal lobe. Schore (2001a) suggests that the maturation of the anterior cingulate is associated with a primary consciousness in human relationships. Regulatory control by the cingulate is based more on the dyadic nature of human social interactions, which can hierarchically override the unitary interactions of the amygdala. Schore (2001a) believes that the growth and maturation of the anterior cingulate is a milestone in brain development, corresponding to the attachment-in-the-making phase suggested by John Bowlby (1969/1982); it is a critical stage for secure attachment.

New Skills

- He likes to play and explore and can sit with support for a longer period of time. You may see him seriously studying toys, and he may begin selecting his favorite toy.

- He still likes to reach for toys and put them in his mouth for exploration. He now may try to scoot or pull himself to get a toy.

- He especially likes to bang toys to hear interesting sounds and feel greater movement.

- He can grab his feet, roll, wiggle, smile, and babble all at the same time, especially if you are interacting with him.

- He is very curious and will look at the floor when an object falls from the table to see what happened to it.

- He can follow your pointing finger and look at what you are showing him.

- His babbling is beginning to sound like the rhythm and tone of speech, and he may make many interesting "comments" while he is playing. His face will also have many expressions as he learns how things work.

- He is at ease with his family and likes his routines; in fact, he can anticipate his routines before they happen.

- He is good-natured, for the most part, and enjoys his world. You may hear him laughing hilariously at something. He may get frustrated and angry, too, when things don't go as expected.

CULTIVATING SECURE ATTACHMENT IN THE SIX-MONTH-OLD

Greater development and complexity in the brain allows the six-month-old to have more time to play and explore, especially when his parents have been consistent enough in responding to his needs and giving him plenty of positive interaction. You can now see his preferences for certain toys. The six-month-old is beginning to show in his behavior the increased complexity in his brain. He understands more than you think, and what he understands is based upon what he has learned nonverbally. The six-month-old is now starting to understand the word "no," because your face and voice change when you use this word. You won't be using this word as often now as you will later, when he starts walking, but, of course, you will occasionally say "no," especially if your baby is about to investigate how milk falls out of a cup! He is beginning to respond to his own name and to other familiar words that describe his routines. It is only when he continually hears a word paired with an event that he will begin to associate the sound of the word with an event; he will also read your face, voice, and touch to help him interpret the significance of the event. In this way, babies understand long before they learn what actual words mean.

So cultivating a secure attachment means continuing with attunement, emotional regulation, and matching your baby's needs for play, exploration, soothing, and rest, as well as responding to his physical needs. Again, what's important is to do a good enough job of regulating your baby's negative emotions while increasing positive emotions. Doing this, you have built in a reliable foundation in your infant that feels like "whatever goes wrong gets fixed." This is the outward foundation for secure attachment. The inner foundation is a regulated nervous system in a brain that has all of its connections. Now it's time to return to Corey and Stephanie to see what adjustment needed to be made.

Corey and Stephanie: Reestablishing Trust

Again, the typically developing six-month-old wants to explore for longer periods of time, likes his routines (for they allow him to begin to anticipate his daily experiences), needs lots and lots of positive play interactions with his parents, and still needs his parents to make the bad feelings go away. Routines are critical in child development in general (even we adults enjoy our routines), but they are particularly important for the six-month-old, for he is starting to anticipate what happens next. He will eventually notice that when you're running the bathwater, getting the duck, and talking with him using the "bath voice," it means playtime in the water! He has noticed all of these nonverbal movements and paired them with your facial expressions and voice and is now putting it all together to understand that a bath is about to happen. See how a baby's development leads to greater complexity?

But Corey and Stephanie were in a misattunement cycle that had the potential of misaligning their relationship, which, of course, could affect Corey's development. Stuff happens with babies—teething, fevers, mishaps, food allergies, and fussiness—creating many a worried moment for parents. Knowing what to do helps, and a good pediatrician can be helpful not only in taking care of the medical issue but also in reassuring parents. For Stephanie, though, the pediatrician's reassurance somehow didn't do the trick. Corey's fussiness because of teething was disturbing to Stephanie. After a couple of sessions, it became clear that Stephanie was not accustomed to ongoing fussiness in Corey. She was able to do a good job of soothing and comforting him during the couple of days he felt lousy after getting his shots, but his teething fussiness seemed to be going "on and on," and this was hard on Stephanie. She began to attribute his fussiness to Corey not liking her anymore, which caused her to make subtle changes in their routines. I learned that Stephanie had been letting her mother give Corey a bath because she didn't want to see his unhappiness. She had also decreased the amount of time she was playing with him, so when she played peekaboo with him, it was more unexpected and he fussed, which, of course, reinforced Stephanie's worry that her baby didn't need her anymore.

Since Stephanie lived with her mother and father, I asked if it would be okay to invite her mother to a session with her. Through her mother's support, Stephanie learned that Corey was fine when he was fussy and that fussiness is typical in development. In fact, fussiness and irritability can occur when a baby (or child) goes into the next developmental stage. (If you doubt this, wait for adolescence!) Although routines may be altered at times because of illness or other unplanned events, maintaining routines provides scaffolding for all emotions, including fussiness.

In fact, healthy routines are very reassuring to children, in general, and will help immensely to iron out a fussiness stage. Routines say to babies something like "even though it all feels bad, it must not be that bad because life seems to be going on as usual." In infancy, this will be not thought but felt, helping your baby learn that even if you feel lousy, life goes on as expected, which has the effect of helping the infant cope. When Stephanie backed out of her routines with Corey, it reinforced his fussiness, for not only did he feel lousy with his gums hurting, but also his mother was disappearing. Stephanie understood this immediately, and in a matter of weeks, their relationship was back on track ... and Corey had a new tooth!

PLAY AND ATTACHMENT IN THE SIX-MONTH-OLD

Six-month-olds are a lot of fun to play with. For the most part, they are easy playmates. One of my former interns came in with her six-month-old boy, who easily played with another intern's hair for almost twenty minutes because she creatively invented many "hair games," like brushing his face with her hair, all the while using exaggerated faces and wonderful, excited voices. When a six-month-old feels excited, he will also babble at you and wiggle his body, showing you how much he loves your positive play interactions. Positive play interactions are fun for everyone, and they amplify everyone's affect. These "vitality affects" (mentioned in chapter 2) are bursts of pleasurable feeling states that are shared and resonant, creating wonderful endorphin cascades in both the baby's and your brain. As you know already, resonance and synchrony have everything to do with bonding and brain development. And it is pretty easy to get into a resonating bubble with a six-month-old.

GAMES: Banging and Exploring Cause and Effect

- Six-month-olds love to explore by reaching, mouthing, and banging toys. If you give your six-month-old a big plastic spoon, he'll probably bang it. Avoid heavy objects, though, as his arm coordination is still wobbly, and he might hit his head with the object in his enthusiasm.

- Peekaboo games are immensely pleasurable for most six-month-olds, who will love it when you hide your eyes with your hands and then take them away, saying "I see you" or "Where's the baby? There you are."

- Even though he won't understand the words yet, your six-month-old will like to look at a lift-the-flap, peekaboo book to find what's missing. He will start to lift the flaps almost immediately.

- He's starting to find the missing item, as he is learning that even though you put a toy behind your back, it still exists, and he may want to reach for it.

- Sitting him on the floor with a big pillow as support and rolling a medium-sized ball toward him is a fun game. He will love this and try to push the ball or pick it up.

- Singing and playing in the bath is immensely fun for most six-month-olds. Your baby may like you dribbling water over his face and down his tummy as a game. Since he will close his eyes when you trickle the water and open them when the water stops running, you can also make it a peekaboo game.

- Blowing bubbles so that he can watch and experience bubbles floating and landing on him is a great game for a six-month-old. He may try to catch one and experience the pop.

- Making up a feeding song, using a zooming movement to get the spoon in his mouth, can also be a fun game, especially for babies who are fussy when eating.

PARENT FOCUS: A NIGHT OFF

Recently, while traveling in Seattle, I got on the hotel elevator with a young couple who had just arrived for the night. I noticed that all they had with them was a small cosmetic case, which the man was carrying. I smiled just to acknowledge the couple, but the man must have been self-conscious about this small traveling case. He began nervously explaining that the woman with him was his wife. I smiled broadly as I took in why they were looking a little sheepish. He then went on to say that they had a seven-month-old and a three-year-old at home with his parents, that this was their first night away in a very long time, that his parents could call them at any time, and that the two of them could, of course, return home, if needed. The explanation would likely have continued on had I not reached my floor! As I got off the elevator, I said, "Have fun," and smiled all the way down the hall.

LIVING IN THE CHARM: RANDY'S GIFT FROM HEAVEN

Randy, a cute seven-month-old, was in his stroller between his mother and father at a crowded soup and salad bar. There were two long lines of people making salads while inching toward the cash register. Randy was banging on the stroller tray, looking up at his mother and father, banging more, looking at the other people in line, energetically waving his arm over his head while opening and clamping his hand (the international "gimme" sign). Unfortunately, the place was so noisy and his parents so intent on the task at hand that no one noticed ... except for Leda, his four-year-old sister, who was trailing behind her dad. She saw what her brother was doing and apparently decided to help out. Standing on her tiptoes, she grabbed hold of an extended spoon in the dish of peas, and before anyone could blink an eye, peas were flying everywhere. Like an answer to a prayer, three landed on Randy's tray, and with a big smile, he promptly picked up one and smashed it on the way to his mouth.

CHAPTER 7

There's a Stranger Amongst Us!
The Nine-Month-Old

Hermit Crab stepped out of the shell and onto the floor of the ocean. But it was frightening out in the open sea without a shell to hide in.
—Eric Carle, *A House for Hermit Crab*

The good-natured easiness of the six-month-old gives way to an infant who is now likely to scrunch her face, turn away, and reach for her parent if you are a stranger trying to say hello. Sometimes when the infant is securely backed up against her parent, she may turn and give you another wary once-over and quickly turn away again. By nine months, infants are generally wary of strangers and feel anxious around people they don't know. This is called *stranger anxiety*, and it is a natural developmental milestone that occurs around seven to nine months. It is occurring because of the infant's increased brain development, which now allows her not only to know who is in her clan but also to know who isn't. This ability is, of course, protective as the infant is getting close to being more mobile, if not already. With greater mobility, the infant can now go to her parents herself, not just signal that she needs a parent to come to her. Among her increasing repertoire of attachment behaviors, the infant will now approach and follow her primary caregivers, especially her mother.

With the onset of locomotion, infants can show their "true intention" because they can follow their mothers when distressed. Ainsworth considered the integration of locomotion and object permanence (knowing the mother exists even if she isn't in sight) to be the phase of "clear-cut attachment" (Ainsworth et al. 1978, 25–26). With the onset of stranger anxiety, the infant's "intention" can be clearly determined as an infant will actively display separation distress and will use attachment behaviors, such as following, reaching to be picked up, and clinging to maintain proximity and contact with her mother. Although attachment behaviors in the form of signaling, such as crying, smiling, and vocalizing, have been present all along, it is easier to see the infant's own intent to maintain contact with her primary caregivers as the infant develops greater mobility. Based upon sensitive and attuned care, parents can help their nine-month-old in the throes of separation anxiety by soothing, reassuring, and helping her to master these now ever-increasing social interactions with others.

Infants can seem more clingy and need more soothing and reassurance during this period. Friends and relatives often need soothing, too, as they try to greet your formerly open and cheery infant, who is now tense and staring at them as if they were baby stealers! Recall in chapter 2, Howard's interaction with his daughter Jessica when I approached her to say good-bye. Jessica was already a year old at the time, but nine-month-olds require similar parental scaffolding. In fact, parents may have to work harder than before to keep their nine-month-old's physiology within optimal ranges, for often the old soothing behaviors don't work quite as well. In this stage of development, redirecting begins to become the magic ring inscribed with the words "You're okay; it's okay."

SETTING THE SCENE: AMY'S STRUGGLE FOR EXPLORATION

Amy was a beautiful nine-month-old who was carried into my office by her father, Michael. Her mother, Vanessa, introduced her to me. Amy cuddled back further into her father's arms and made a slight turning away but did give a semi-smile from this position. Michael and Vanessa had come for a consultation because they were concerned that their different parenting styles were confusing for Amy. After a few awkward moments, Michael revealed that he came in because he believed that Vanessa's approach to Amy was "chaotic," but quickly added that she was a good mother. Vanessa quickly responded that she felt Michael was "too rigid."

I suggested that they put the baby on a blanket on the floor if she were willing. She wouldn't go at first, but some interesting toys caught her eye and she eventually wanted down. Amy sat well on the blanket and fingered a pop-up toy consisting of plastic eggs and levers. If you push the levers, ducklings pop out of the eggs. As we talked about what "chaotic" and "too rigid" meant for this family, Michael got on the floor and pushed the levers so that Amy could see the pop-ups. He then took her hand and pushed it down on the levers, I assumed so that she could see for herself how it worked. She reached for the stacking rings. Michael quickly took all the rings off the column, held each one in front of her eyes, and then reassembled the rings. After this, he undid the rings again and handed Amy the biggest ring to put on the column. Amy reached for the nearest ring (a smaller one) and began to study it. Michael then said, "No, Amy. This one goes first, see?" Amy hesitantly picked up another ring. Several issues stood out:

1. Michael appeared to play with Amy because he wanted to distract himself from the difficult conversation with Vanessa.

2. Vanessa did not seem to notice when Michael dropped out of the conversation.

3. Amy did not vocalize, and her exploration appeared to be dampened by Michael's play interaction. She also made no eye contact with Michael and only briefly glanced at her mother.

As a therapist, I often find that men are surprised to discover that their true feelings are valued and even sought after in therapy, for unfortunately, the socialization process still encourages men to believe that expressing feelings is somehow unmanly. William Pollack (1998) has much to say about this in his book entitled *Real Boys*. When I asked Michael if he agreed with what Vanessa was saying, he returned to the couch and contributed more to the conversation. I'll return to Amy, Vanessa, and Michael when I discuss secure attachment in nine-month-olds, but first here's a look at the typical physical, social-emotional, and brain development for this age group.

DEVELOPMENTAL MILESTONES: BUILDING CONNECTION AS YOUR BABY GROWS

Nine-month-olds expect responses to be predictable, as they have had quite a lot of experience now with their parents, family members, routines, and play. You may notice your nine-month-old is now orienting to familiar words like "bottle" or "ba-ba," "Mama," or "Dada." She is continuing to learn about how the world works but knows a lot already. For example, all that reading to your infant has paid off, because now when you sit her on your lap with a book, she will likely want to turn the pages herself and look at the pictures. She may even point to a picture, which will probably prompt you to name the picture for her. Nine-month-olds will also mimic what you do, so if you are waving good-bye to a friend, your baby may try to wave good-bye too. This generally prompts parents to say "wave bye-bye," creating the beautiful and intricate mini-step dance of baby imitating, parent identifying and naming, and baby refining and mastering.

Your Baby's Physical and Social-Emotional Development

In general, the nine-month-old can do the following:

- Sit without support for up to ten to fifteen minutes.

- Crawl or creep and may be starting to pull up to a stand. If she is pulling up, you might see that she can also walk sideways.

- Take steps if you hold both her hands and guide her.

- Use her thumb and index finger (a pincer grasp) to grasp a small item like a Cheerio.

- Imitate sounds and gestures.

- Vocalize several different consonant-vowel combinations when she jabbers.

- Gesture to make her needs known.

- Actively look at pictures in books and turn pages.

- Put her finger into a small hole, so that baby proofing the house is now critical.

- Recognize names of familiar objects and understand the word "no." She may express hurt and have trouble coping with limits, however.

- Look for an object that she sees you hide, as she is learning about object permanence.

Your Baby's Brain Development

The growth of synapses and the myelination of axons continue at a vigorous rate, maturing and connecting the limbic system with cortical association areas. Synaptic growth and pruning are occurring side by side as a way of organizing and reorganizing what the baby is learning. Although genetic scaffolding supports the unfolding of critical periods of growth in particular areas of an infant's brain as she matures, the overall organization of her brain reflects her lived experience with her primary caregivers. The primary focus of growth continues to be in the right hemisphere, the goal being to connect and mature the right orbitofrontal cortex, the area of the brain that's involved in higher levels of motivation and emotional regulation. This doesn't mean that the left hemisphere is not operating, but, rather, that the dominant area for growth is still the right hemisphere. The critical period for development of the orbitofrontal cortex begins at ten to twelve months and continues well into the second year of life (Schore 2000).

Continued maturation of the anterior cingulate and other associated structures allows the infant to integrate visual material with tone of voice and touch. The infant will now have more awareness of another's attitude (Schore 2001a). An increased ability to share attentional states with primary caregivers can result in "shared mind" states, or what Tronick (2007, 3) calls "dyadic states of consciousness," which are immensely satisfying to the infant and are important for not only increased consciousness but emotional security.

Schore (2001a) suggests that stranger anxiety represents the PNS maturation of the cingulate and that PNS maturation comes after the earlier SNS maturation of the cingulate. Remember that the cingulate has connections into the autonomic nervous system and acts as a higher regulatory control center over the amygdala when dyadic interactions are good enough. Because the infant now has greater awareness of others, and the PNS has inhibitory functions, the unfamiliar can create negative states in the infant's body, triggering defensive behavior. This evolutionary advance coincides with the infant's greater mobility and serves to inhibit her approach to people she doesn't know, thus protecting the infant and prompting her to return to her primary caregivers.

New Skills

- She likes to imitate what you do and see what you are looking at. If you clap your hands together, she will want to do the same. She loves to wave bye-bye, with your prompting, and will learn to vocalize "bye-bye" too.

- She likes to pick up small pieces of food on her tray and feed herself. She may also like drinking from a sippy cup.

- She will look for an object you hide if she sees you hide it, as she knows that "just because you can't see it, doesn't mean it's not there."

- She can point to what she is interested in or what she wants you to see.

- She can have a comfort toy like a "blankie" that she may want with her and will resist giving up.

- She can sit by herself and play with toys and move into a crawl or creep to get a toy. She may be pulling up to a stand as well. She can also take steps when adults are holding her hands.

- She can have jabbering conversations filled with consonant-vowel combinations. She loves when you speak to her and tell her she has a lot to say!

- She can play cooperatively in simple games like clapping and ball rolling. She especially loves well-known games where she can predict the ending, like "Kitchey, Kitchey, Coo."

- She also likes pulling things apart to see how they work and will look for objects she hears but doesn't see.

CULTIVATING SECURE ATTACHMENT IN THE NINE-MONTH-OLD

By nine months, your baby can now actively follow you if she is crawling. Even though nine-month-olds are never far away, you can see the natural venturing-out-and-coming-back movement of development, now that your baby is more mobile. Returning to you functions not only as a shared moment of experience but also as emotional refueling for safety and security, which continues to balance and regulate her emotional world, freeing her to explore again. In nine-month-olds, this concentric movement may consist of your baby shifting her attention onto a toy, followed by presenting the toy to you. When you comment about the toy or say "thank you," she feels your shared participation in her play. Often babies have another expectation when they present a toy to you. That is, they want it back! When attunement has been sensitive and good enough, you will see before your eyes how your baby is using you as a secure base from which to explore. If tired, hungry, or irritable, she knows she can go to you, for you can make her feel better. When she needs play, she knows that a neat game will appear. When she needs a cuddle, she knows she will get one. She is neither afraid to approach you nor afraid to leave you to explore. This is a trust built directly from her experience with you; it is this trust that is forming a secure attachment, which can be reliably measured in just three more months. Now that you know more about what a typically developing nine-month-old looks like, what was amiss with Amy, Michael, and Vanessa?

Amy, Michael, and Vanessa: Establishing Confidence in Each Other

Again, a typically developing nine-month-old will explore on her own while sitting for a while and will likely jabber if she feels secure enough. She also likes to play with her parents and will imitate much of what they do. Since we also know that a nine-month-old can be leery of strangers and newness in general, which can affect her vocalizations and her play, it was not clear initially how to interpret Amy's diminished play and vocalizations. But what was atypical, even under the circumstances, was for Amy to have no eye contact with her father when he was so close to her.

As it turned out, the more we worked together, the clearer it became that Michael felt very little acceptance from Vanessa and was turning to Amy to reduce his frustration and to feel better. He also felt their lives had become increasingly chaotic since they'd had Amy and believed that this had more to do with Vanessa's "chaotic nature" than with Amy. Vanessa, on the other hand, felt constantly criticized by Michael and tended to give what I call a "teach-and-correct" response, suggesting that he needed to "lighten up and understand that life with babies is not neat." This confusing communication problem between her parents sometimes spilled over onto Amy, in that during a tense interaction between the couple, Michael might suddenly approach Amy to focus on a teach-and-correct play interaction with her.

As the therapy advanced, I was able to ask Michael if it was hard to stay engaged in the conversation with Vanessa, as he continued to seek out Amy when the conversation got tough. He eventually was able to acknowledge this pattern in himself and felt he went to Amy as a way of calming down. As Michael and Vanessa worked through their relationship differences, they began to have more confidence in each other. They set aside some adult time alone together and agreed on some routines to increase the order in the home (even with an infant). Michael became more aware of his critical side and realized that he got increasingly critical in an attempt to control his own anger and emotional reactivity. Vanessa also learned that her teach-and-correct approach stemmed from how incompetent she felt when Michael criticized her; it was an attempt to control her own feelings of inadequacy. Michael also learned how to give Amy more space to explore before introducing new ways to use toys. He was also encouraged to use more interactive games with Amy, like hiding something in front of her or rolling a ball, to amplify her play. When the therapy ended, Amy was eighteen months old. Seeing her develop while her parents were improving their relationship was wonderful. She became an adorable toddler who showed healthy *agency*, that is, a natural ability to make her wants and interests known.

PLAY AND ATTACHMENT IN THE NINE-MONTH-OLD

Nine-month-olds have a lot of understanding of family and social inter-actions and may already be requesting various items, foods, or people, as they point or use consonant-vowel words that parents are learning to figure out. Providing the words for your infant's vocalizations or gestures not only helps her hear more language but also lets her know that you understand her. Nine-month-olds continue to love interaction, and now that they can use gestures, their communication is more understand-able. For example, when nine-month-old Mia pointed to the family dog and said "Pa," her mother responded by saying, "Yes, that's Pepe!" Her mother then asked, "Where's Pepe?" whereupon Mia responded with more pointing.

Nine-month-olds will now initiate interaction with you and might present a toy to hold or invite you to play with a block. All of these play interactions are embedded within your ongoing relationship that has been built upon lived experience. Even though your nine-month-old may show the hesitancy or clinginess of stranger anxiety, moving closer to your infant to help her with her wariness will allow her to use the security of your relationship to master this stage.

GAMES: Hiding, Finding, and Imitating

- Nine-month-olds love to imitate what you do, so if you are waving good-bye to someone, expect your nine-month-old to do it too. Clapping games are also fun, especially when you clap after she pushes a ball back to you or copies you putting a block in a slot.

- Listening to music, singing, and moving with the music can be a lot of fun for your baby. You may find that she has a favorite song.

- Toys with different textures are fun for your nine-month-old. You may find that she now has a favorite toy or blanket that she wants with her.

- She likes hiding games, especially when she sees you hide the object. Your crawling infant will like you to hide behind a chair and ask her, "Where's Mommy?" as long as you don't jump out at her when she finds you.

- Reading her favorite books to her is very comforting and entertaining, as she is becoming quite familiar with what comes on the next page. Having puppets read the book can be fascinating for her.

- Walking barefoot in the grass while holding your hands or in a puddle can be a wonderful experience for your nine-month-old (as long as there are no harmful objects around).

- She will love to open a box to find an object you hid inside that makes a sound. An oatmeal box will do just fine.

- Having you name what she points to is a wonderful game. It is especially fun for her if you can figure out when her pointing means that she wants something and you help her get it. She will also like it when you point at things and tell her what they are.

PARENT FOCUS: FAMILY VACATIONS

The Monterey Peninsula is a wonderful vacation spot for families. There's the beach as well as many other attractions for both adults and children to enjoy. During the summer months, parents pushing strollers with children draped over them are seen everywhere. One morning, as I was having breakfast at an inn, a family of five strolled in. Sean was carrying four-month-old Ross, followed by two-and-a-half-year-old Eva, five-year-old Val, and their mom, Olivia.

As I had my breakfast, I watched as Sean and Olivia talked with each other, easily breaking away from their adult conversation when Val threw his napkin on the floor. Olivia calmly said to Val, "We don't throw napkins on the floor," as Sean looked on. Val picked up the napkin. As Eva slipped between the open arms of the chair (deliberately), Sean, who was still holding Ross, readjusted her. Eva, feeling this was a wonderful game, tried it again.

It's a wonderful family indeed when the adults are easy enough with their children to include their own relationship. All too often when kids are with their parents the focus is solely on the kids, which is not good for the adults or the children. Children feel more secure knowing that their parents value their relationship with each other, as long as they also know that when they need their parent, he or she can easily tune in. Sean and Olivia were relaxed with their family and continued to have an adult boundary for their relationship that they could count on. They moved easily from their own relationship to the family, to an individual child, back to the family, then to their relationship, with such naturalness, good humor, and calmness that their sense of belonging was seeable. Not only did their children belong to them, but Sean and Olivia belonged to each other, and their primary relationship was present even with the children.

LIVING IN THE CHARM: KARA FINDS HER BEAT!

Nine-month-old Kara was sitting in a high chair at a family reunion held at a restaurant. She was the first second-generation child born into this family, so she was surrounded by ten adults, including her parents. As the adults were ordering dinner and talking with each other, Kara suddenly started wiggling and hopping up and down with such intensity that the adults stopped immediately to see if she was okay. After a moment, her startled parents could see that she was dancing on her own to the music that was playing in the background.

CHAPTER 8

Free at Last:
The Twelve-Month-Old

*Little Guy runs away so fast. Little Guy's daddy has
to run like anything just to catch that baby up.*
—Vera Williams, *"More, More, More," Said the Baby*

Much has changed in your baby's development now that he is twelve
months old. You may have baked his first birthday cake and watched
as he grabbed a nice handful to put in his mouth! Your baby is likely
walking or will be soon and is now constantly everywhere at once. Your
formerly eclectic living-room coffee table has taken on a minimalist look
as you have come to learn that those nice pieces of art are also interesting to your upright child. He can now move away from you to explore,
and this freedom generally comes with much happiness and excitement.
There is nothing cuter than hearing the laughter of a newly upright infant
running and squealing with delight as his parent lumbers after him.

The psychoanalyst Margaret Mahler (Mahler, Pine, and Bergman 1975) calls this phase of development a *practicing period* that begins when the infant is able to move (crawl and walk) around on his own, generally the period between nine and sixteen months. As young as two months old, infants can show an increased interest in the outside world, and this interest is easily identified by four months. But when infants are able to move around on their own, it greatly increases their exploration away from their parents. This change in development is thought to be the earliest phase of identity formation, as the infant is experiencing himself as independent (he thinks!) from the parent and is now quite full of himself, which is healthy. Mahler calls this the beginning of the *separation-individuation phase* (Mahler, Pine, and Bergman 1975). Of course, this is also the phase when socialization begins for the infant who is mobile and can get into everything. Infants can now *visually reference* their parents; that is, they will look at the parent's face from where they are to see if everything is still okay. They will also quickly move back to the parent if they are afraid, tired, hungry, or just in need of a cuddle for reassurance, or what Mahler calls a "refueling" (Mahler, Pine, and Bergman 1975). You will likely find that your baby quickly moves toward you if you try to leave. Because of this rhythmic developmental movement of traveling away from the parent for exploration and back again for emotional refueling, your child's attachment bond to you can be easily seen (and measured). Your child's security is noticeable now as he will seek you out if he is afraid and won't leave you until he feels reassured. Once he has this reassurance, off he goes again to explore, which is the hallmark of security.

SETTING THE SCENE: MAX'S ATTEMPTS TO TAKE CARE OF HIS MOTHER

You may recall from chapter 2 that I supervise a large program for homeless children and their families at St. Vincent de Paul Village. The children range in age from birth to five years old. Because of the extreme stresses of homelessness, we evaluate all children under five so that we can provide as much developmental support for the child and his family as possible. Single mothers head up most of the families. The story of

Max and his mother shows how typical developmental rhythms can be derailed because of circumstance. The same phenomenon can also be seen in children who have a depressed primary caregiver.

Max was an adorable twelve-month-old boy with a lot of hair who came in for his evaluation with his mother, Jane. As is true for many a homeless child, he was elated to see that the room had toys. Using the testing toys, he immediately began to play with the examiner, while I talked with his mother about his development. Max came from a home where he had witnessed domestic violence, and his mother had just recently made the decision to leave. Max had not seen his father for a month prior to testing.

Max loved working with the blocks and enthusiastically put all of them in a cup. He also was imitating the examiner's movements well and was completely absorbed with putting pegs in a pegboard. During the developmental interview with Jane, which was occurring across the room, Jane began to cry because of the trauma of her life. Max immediately left the pegboard and came up to her and began rubbing her leg. He also was looking directly at her face. He then began to climb up on her, even without her making an offer to pick him up, and put his head on her shoulder. Jane helped him up, saying, "I'm all right baby. It's okay, I'm just a little sad right now." A couple of issues stood out:

1. Jane had been through much trauma and was doing her best to support Max, but she was in need of multiple services and immediate support.

2. Max also showed us that he was significantly traumatized as well, as he completely left his own developmental process to take care of his mother.

Max's attempt to regulate his mother's emotions was a survival strategy. This points to an important topic. Many adults seeking psychotherapy come from environments where their social-emotional development was compromised because they either had to care for and/or be watchful of their parents at an early age. The circumstances do not have to be as extreme as those encountered by Max. The issue of "who is regulating whom" can occur in more typical home environments where there might be an environmental trauma, such as a divorce, a significant death, or severe depression. The questions "what is your child learning?" and "whose needs are being met?" will be particularly helpful when considering the complexity involved in emotional regulation under these circumstances. Children are resilient by nature, but it is important to understand when "too much" derails development. I will return to Max and Jane when I discuss secure attachment in twelve-month-olds, but first here's a look at what is typical physical, social-emotional, and brain development for this age group.

DEVELOPMENTAL MILESTONES: BUILDING CONNECTION AS YOUR BABY GROWS

If you look carefully, you will see how skills and interests from other stages are still present, only now they have expanded into more complexity. Now that your walking infant is mobile, he may want to try more advanced imitations when he watches you cook. Adding real household objects to his toy chest like a plastic bowl and spatula will now allow him to "cook" with you. You may find him sitting on the kitchen floor and mixing something of his own. Although your twelve-month-old understands more than he can speak, he will generally be able to use two or three words now and use them correctly. Often these first important words are what he needs the most, such as "Mama," "Dada," and some word for bottle. But he will still excitedly gesture if he wants you to see something. Routines are still important, but you may find that since your infant can walk, he may resist going down for a nap or going to bed, as it is way too much fun to play, and he doesn't want to miss anything. This is where your well-established routines pay off, for if you can get him into the routine, the familiarity will help settle him down.

Your Baby's Physical and Social-Emotional Development

In general, the twelve-month-old can do the following:

- Stand, squat, and walk, and now he may not want to sit down! If he is walking on his own, he can also walk with you if you hold his hand. He also may be pushing to a stand from a squat, all while holding on to a toy!

- Throw a ball and explore objects using pushing, spinning, and rolling movements. In fact, he may prefer objects that move.

- Hammer pegs and play with blocks. You can see the difference in his play now that he can more easily explore, which is quite different from his earlier stage when he would simply bang his toys.

- Grasp a pencil at its far end (and may be learning how to grasp it in the middle) and scribble on a paper. He can also sit at a child table in a child-sized chair.

- Solve simple problems like how to use a stick to get a toy out of a tight spot or put one object in each hand and a third under his arm when he wants to carry all three.

- Imitate what you do, and if it is so cute that you laugh, don't be surprised if he repeats what he did just to get you to laugh again.

- "Sing" with you by moving, dancing, or clapping.

- Open cabinets, doors, and boxes and take everything out. Baby proofing any low entry cabinet is critical.

- Be generally affectionate and give you toys on a regular basis.

- Play alongside another child, called *parallel play*, but does not play interactively with another child yet.

- Begin to show a temper when he can't have his way.

Your Baby's Brain Development

Your baby's brain is growing at a phenomenal rate. Like a rheostat that can increase the lighting in your dining room, your baby's brain power has greatly increased with connections now being made to the orbitofrontal cortex. According to Schore (1994, 2001a), the maturation of the orbitofrontal cortex goes through a critical growth period beginning around ten months and extending into the second year of life. With its deep connections to other limbic structures like the anterior cingulate and amygdala, as well as to the SNS and the PNS, the orbitofrontal cortex is thought to be the highest regulatory center in the brain for emotions (Schore 2001a). The right orbitofrontal cortex has been found to be involved in human social interactions, arousal and mood regulation, and motivational and planning states (Schore 2001a). It appears to process and compare incoming information from the outside world with feedback coming from the interior body world and modulate emotions and behavior to support motivation and learning (Schore 2000). The right orbitofrontal cortex processes incoming information at lightning speed. A well-connected orbitofrontal cortex can override the appraisals of the lower limbic structures and "act as an executive control function for the entire right brain" (Schore 2000, 31).

Schore (1996) points out that there are two orbitofrontal-midbrain-limbic circuits, one of which is excitatory and is involved in positive emotions, behavioral approaches, and rewards. The other is inhibitory and involved with negative emotions, behavioral inhibition, and aversive outcomes (see chapter 9). High levels of endorphins directly act on the excitatory circuit and increase SNS arousal levels, giving the infant immensely pleasurable feelings. Heightened levels of SNS activation in the practicing-phase infant are not only activating this excitatory circuit but also contributing to the infant's sense of elation (Schore 1996).

New Skills

- He loves to be upright and will either pull up on furniture or walk on his own. He also will naturally squat to pick up something he's interested in.

- He likes to communicate what he wants, using his gestures and the few words he knows, but if you get it wrong, he will let you know.

- He may be responding to one-step requests, like "go get your shoes."

- He wants to do everything that you do, so if his dad is in the garage hammering something together, he will want to take his hammer-and-peg set and make something too.

- He will work to solve a problem, like removing a lid so he can see what's making the noise inside.

- He may "sing" parts of his favorite song with you and even attempt to say some of the words.

- He can put a puzzle piece into an infant puzzle board. He can pick up blocks and put them in a container too.

- He can build by putting two blocks on top of each other and find a toy you hide under one of two cups, even if you reverse the position of the cups.

- He can identify many pictures he sees in familiar bedtime books if you ask him to show you.

CULTIVATING SECURE ATTACHMENT IN THE TWELVE-MONTH-OLD

Even though your twelve-month-old feels like he's on top of the world, more than ever he needs his parents to help regulate his emotions. For the twelve-month-old, this usually means help with down-regulating his natural high from moving and exploring. Parents may find the word "no" slipping out of their mouths more often than they think as their infant finds more interesting things to do on his own. Focusing on a one-step request or redirection can be a life-saver, especially when you put it in the form of a question. Remember seventeen-month-old Alfonso, whose prolonged, hilarious play with the balloon triggered his parents to down-regulate this state? To divert his attention away from the balloon, Alfonso's mother put his sippy cup on the coffee table and asked him if he wanted a drink. This form of asking a question to redirect a child's attention generally works well during this phase of development. It is also relational, so the redirection is riding on the secure relationship that you have already built with your child. Now that you know more about what a typically developing twelve-month-old looks like, it's time to return to Max and Jane.

Max and Jane: Finding Safety

A typical twelve-month-old will move away from his parents to explore and return when he is afraid, hungry, tired, or just in need of emotional refueling. This typical pattern was greatly derailed in Max, for though he moved easily into exploration, he immediately left exploration to soothe his mother. During the evaluation period and subsequent dyadic play therapy, I never saw him returning to his mother for his own comfort and reassurance. In fact, I saw just the opposite. He approached his mother only when trying to comfort and reassure her. He was incredibly tuned in to her emotional state, not for his own developmental needs for refueling and exploration but rather for survival. Max had developed a survival strategy that had more to do with keeping his mother regulated, which then gave his mother the best opportunity to care for him.

His mother, who was struggling with her own emotions, appeared to reinforce Max's attempts to soothe her, as these were times when she was warm and caring. When he played, she basically left him alone. The strategy that Max was developing went something like "if I soothe mother, she will be loving and take care of me." This, of course, is not conscious but is a feeling encoded into implicit memory as a pattern for how relationships work. He was also using a complete stranger as a base from which to explore. This is an atypical response for a twelve-month-old and if it continued to occur regularly, it would affect the trajectory of Max's overall development. As it was, Max had not yet developed any words. He did gesture occasionally, but his mother did not respond when he did. He basically played alone but would interact with anyone who seemed to have an interest in him.

Max and Jane were given a dyadic play therapy to work on these issues. Jane also received many other services, including her own individual therapy, legal advice, and a healthy-relationships group. She also received other career and education services. To enhance treatment, we commonly videotape therapy sessions, with the parent's consent, and then review the video with the parent to highlight his or her strengths. In this case, Jane's intern clinician was able to highlight how warm and loving Jane was with Max when Jane was sad and how sensitive Max was to her feelings. The intern was also able to ask her about her feelings when Max played alone. Jane felt happy for her son that he was able to play and seemed surprised when the intern asked if she ever wanted to play with him.

We were able to work with this family for nine sessions. As is typical of many homeless residents, they left spontaneously. By then, however, Jane had greater awareness of how her emotions were pulling Max away from his exploring. She also had seen on video that Max did show signs of needing her reassurance. We suggested to Jane that when Max tried to sit in the therapist's lap, he needed comforting or refueling himself and that we believed he really wanted to sit in his mother's lap. In a flash of awareness, Jane said, "Oh yes," and during the next session asked Max if he wanted to sit on her lap. He did. At the last session, Jane was playing on the floor with Max, who welcomed her.

PLAY AND ATTACHMENT IN THE TWELVE-MONTH-OLD

The twelve-month-old loves movement, of course, now that he can get around. His brain is also making the important connections to the highest control center in the limbic system, allowing him more planning, studied attention, and increased motivation to investigate. Playing with him can include all the ways something can be used. For example, at an infant gym, twelve-month-old Elias crawled and walked through tunnels, sat in a plastic tire, and flopped onto a big ball. His father tilted the tire so it could roll, which was thrilling for Elias, who then pushed the tire around the room. Although Elias was the one actively exploring each item, he was exploring within his secure relationship with his dad. If something were to occur like a slip or a fall, he knew his dad would respond. Even for the temperamentally shy child, having his parent help him explore something new serves to strengthen his secure attachment.

GAMES: Exploring Space

- Twelve-month-olds love to explore new things. If an oversized package was delivered to your house, and the large empty box is now lying on the floor, expect to find your child in it.

- He likes to have the tools to do what you are doing. If he sees you brush your hair, he will likely want to brush his hair too.

- Figuring out how to get something open to see what's inside is a wonderful game for your twelve-month-old. You may find him studying the contents once he has the box open.

- Hide-and-seek games are a lot of fun at this age, as the twelve-month-old may begin "hiding" under a sheet. You can play along, asking "where is he?" or "what happened to him?" Don't be surprised if you hear a giggle coming from beneath the sheet.

- A fun game for him is for you to read to his favorite teddy bear or stuffed animal. You may find that your twelve-month-old pulls the teddy onto his lap, the way you read to him.

- Singing songs to him, especially those with physical movements, like "Itsy-Bitsy Spider" or "The Wheels on the Bus," is wonderful for a twelve-month-old, who will try to copy all your moves.

- He will enjoy you asking him to point to various pictures in his books when you read to him, for he can find many of the pictures you name. You can also emphasize the color of what he points to.

- Water play is a lot of fun at this age, and your twelve-month-old may love his bath. If he is outside, you may find him sitting in a puddle.

PARENT FOCUS: A DAY AT THE AMUSEMENT PARK

Audrey and June were both hardworking single mothers who couldn't really afford a proper vacation. They cleverly decided to join forces and take their children on some day trips together. They told their kids what they had planned and gave the kids some choice in picking which place they could try first. With some planning, Audrey and June coordinated their work schedules and took their combined five kids to Knott's Berry Farm. The youngest child, a twelve-month-old, was alternately carried, rolled around in a stroller, or helped to walk with the two adults each holding a hand. While waiting in line for the Calico train ride, the oldest child, who was about nine, decided to wade in the two-inch stream of water that was flowing nearby. She stepped in, shoes and all. Well, of course, this started a chain reaction, and soon all of the children were in the water, including the twelve-month-old, who single-handedly steered two adults to the stream, so he could put his shoes in too! The two tribes were happy together, and everyone seemed to be enjoying their outing. For Audrey and June, it was also relaxing to share watching the kids and have some adult time as well.

LIVING IN THE CHARM: AUGUST'S SOCIAL PROTOCOL

Twelve-month-old August was playing with his aunt in the yard. She squatted down in front of him to be at his eye level. August promptly moved to her side and squatted too. Now August and his aunt were squatting together, side by side in the yard, with his surprised aunt trying to figure out something they could do together from this new position.

CHAPTER 9

I Think, Therefore I Am:

The Eighteen-Month-Old

"Oh, my," said the Little Blue Engine.
"I'm not very big. And I've never been over
the mountain. But I will try."
—Watty Piper, *The Little Engine That Could*

The elation seen in the twelve-month-old gives way to a more moody child who is now a toddler. In fact, hesitancy and wariness can return as your eighteen-month-old displays a greater range of feelings than before. You may take your excited eighteen-month-old to a birthday party only to find her glued to your side! Or find her declaring that some of the birthday toys are "mine!" In fact, "mine" is a well-used word in the toddler stage, for toddlers like to have their own way. As your toddler's vocabulary expands to include two-word sentences, her language will take on a peculiar commanding quality, as she makes her way through her world requesting "more milk!" and so on. The toddler phase can be a challenging time, as the eighteen-month-old's increased interests and movement naturally trigger parental limits. You may feel that a new style of parenting is needed as your eighteen-month-old starts to become familiar with the word "no." Expanding how you interact with her to include a few tricks of the trade will help immensely, as your own emotions can be quite swayed by the toddler who forcibly refuses to comply one minute only to break down in tears the next. Many a parent has been tossed about on the sea of toddler emotions. Luckily, there are some lifesavers that will help.

The eighteen-month-old is beginning a period of separation and individuation that Margaret Mahler (Mahler, Pine, and Bergman 1975) calls the *rapprochement period*, a period when the toddler is becoming more aware that she is separate from her parents. This important phase occurs between sixteen and twenty-four months and has to do with her developing sense of self. It is a time when the young toddler may again want her mother more often. According to Mahler, the elation from the practicing period changes to more anxiety and fearfulness as the exploring toddler becomes more aware of her separateness. However, this leads to a conflict between wanting to be dependent and independent at the same time, which often looks and feels like ambivalence. Anger and aggression can quickly erupt and are often directed more toward the mother, even when the toddler still needs comfort from her mother. Fathers play a more active role during this tumultuous eruption of the developing self, in helping to regulate these very intense emotions. Mothers may begin to feel that the toddler prefers her dad during this stage, and many a father will tease his wife with "she's perfectly fine with me." Not to worry, Mom. This is nature's way of beginning to move your child into the bigger world.

SETTING THE SCENE: MORGAN'S TERROR

Morgan was a beautiful but sad-appearing eighteen-month-old toddler who was brought to my office by her mother, Deborah. She did not smile or talk but did go over to the toy section of the office and pick up toys. Morgan's father, Will, was out of the country for business and not expected back for a few weeks. Deborah was concerned about Morgan's adjustment to returning home after living with her aunt Margaret in another state for six weeks. Deborah was still recovering from a serious illness that had put her in the hospital for some time. Morgan was sixteen and a half months old when her mother was hospitalized. Although Will was able to be home during some of the hospital time, he needed to return to his business travel for financial reasons. Under the circumstances, they had decided to have Morgan stay with Deborah's sister until life settled down again.

Deborah had previously revealed that Morgan seemed different since she had returned. Deborah initially thought Morgan was just getting used to being home but now said it had been several weeks and Morgan acted like "she doesn't know me." She said, "She follows me around, stares at me, doesn't play with her toys much, and seems dazed. When I go to hug her, she pushes me away." Deborah tried putting her in child care for a few hours a day, thinking that she missed being with other children, since Margaret had other children who had played with Morgan. But Deborah reported that at child care, Morgan had been aggressive with kids and had actually bitten another child. Several issues stood out:

1. Although better, Deborah was still recovering and her former energy had not fully returned.

2. Will, who kept in phone contact, had been absent from his family for long periods of time throughout Morgan's life. His typical travel pattern included four to six weeks out of the country, returning home for two weeks, and then leaving again.

3. Morgan appeared to have detached from her mother; that is, her attachment bond to her mother had been severely disturbed.

The eighteen-month-old is entering a new all-at-once scary and exciting stage that is chock-full of conflict as her parents help to make her feel secure while she works out her needs for dependence and her needs for independence. Going through a separation from her primary attachment figure is particularly difficult at this stage, especially if the separation is prolonged, as it was for Morgan. It's important to remember, too, that the eighteen-month-old is still a very young, sensitive child who is just beginning to experience internal conflict. Much reassurance and encouragement is needed from her parents so that she feels confident and capable, for she now is also experiencing prohibitions, as her parents begin limiting her activities. Feelings of shame will occur anywhere from twelve to eighteen months, with small doses generally seen as part of the typical socialization process (Schore 1994). Shame, however, is a marked inhibitor that automatically brings arousal to lower levels. When too much shame is experienced during this phase, it can greatly affect a child's confidence. I will return to Morgan, Deborah, and Will when I discuss secure attachment in eighteen-month-olds, but first here's a look at typical physical, social-emotional, and brain development for children in this age group.

DEVELOPMENTAL MILESTONES: BUILDING CONNECTION AS YOUR TODDLER GROWS

Although your new toddler is starting to talk more, the primary developmental need for this period is still right-brain regulation. You will be building off of your ongoing relationship with your child, who will still turn to you when life goes awry. She needs you to provide regulation and security for her intense emotions and new experiences so that she can continue exploring and learning without getting toppled by fears and disappointments. Parents work hard during the toddler years, as they continually are regulating their toddler's emotional ups and downs while trying to keep up with her natural curiosity. It is like going through the rapids with its moments of thrill and scare, followed by calm, and then into another fast-moving experience. A well-traveled toddler stage, however, gives way to a preschooler who is beginning to have a modicum of her own emotional regulation. You can look back on this stage and say, "Wow, what a ride!" So, here's a look at what your developing eighteen-month-old can do; bear in mind that the following list is meant to cover a six-month period, from eighteen to twenty-four months.

Your Toddler's Physical and Social-Emotional Development

In general, the eighteen-month-old can do the following:

- Run, but may have a harder time stopping! She can also jump, stand on one foot, walk sideways and backwards.

- Put together a simple puzzle board with triangle, square, and circle shapes. She can also put differently shaped blocks into their correct slots.

- Feed herself using a spoon, as well as drink from a straw.

- Watch what you do and then try it herself. She understands most of what you say now.

- Name some body parts if you point to them and name some pictures.

- Use two-word sentences, know her name, recognize herself in a mirror, and refer to herself as "me." She may be using three-word sentences. She may have a spoken vocabulary of ten to twenty or more words but will understand several hundred words.

- Enjoy "pretend" play and may want to dress up in your clothes or shoes.

- Talk to herself while she plays and act out story themes with her toys, even if you're not sure what the story is!

- Comfort another child or a parent if she feels the person is in distress.

- Have a hard time sharing, but this is still a good time to help her learn to share. She can also participate in cleanup routines.

- Get aggressive and hit or throw things if frustrated or mad.

Your Toddler's Brain Development

Continued maturation of the orbitofrontal cortex and other primary brain sites is occurring, providing a whole brain integration period, which allows your toddler to have symbolic thought. This allows your toddler to do "pretend" play and to use objects symbolically. For example, your toddler may find an interesting bowl and put it on her head for a hat. She now also has more awareness of other people's minds. In a famous study, Repacholi and Gopnik (1997) presented goldfish crackers and broccoli to fourteen-month-olds and eighteen-month-olds to eat. Of course, they all preferred the goldfish crackers. Then the researchers ate a few of the goldfish crackers but said "yuck" and made a disgusted face, indicating they didn't like them. When they ate the broccoli, they said "yum" and smiled. Then the researchers indicated that they wanted some more food. They found that the eighteen-month-olds gave them the broccoli (the food the researchers preferred) even when these children preferred the goldfish. The fourteen-month-olds offered them the goldfish crackers, the food that they liked. This lovely study shows the incredible change occurring in your toddler's thinking skills.

In chapter 8, I also mentioned that there were two important orbito-frontal-midbrain-limbic circuits: one excitatory, involved in positive emotions, behavioral approaches, and rewards; the other inhibitory, involved with negative emotions, behavioral inhibition, and aversive outcomes (Schore 1996). Chapter 8 emphasized the excitatory circuit during the glow of the practicing phase. During the rapprochement period of separation and individuation, however, the inhibitory circuit is greatly emphasized, because of the natural need to inhibit a new toddler's curiosity, possessiveness, and behavior. When parents inhibit their toddler's desires, the PNS is activated to down-regulate the SNS, thus strengthening this cortical-limbic connection. Within a secure relationship with their toddler, parents are actively down-regulating the SNS. The new toddler, however, continues to rely on her parent to bring her back to a balanced emotional state without too much fuss so that she can soon get back to her exploring. A balance between these two circuits, tipped more toward the excitatory circuit, means that the toddler is having more positive feelings and experiences than negative, and this is important for future development. Since the orbitofrontal cortex can override the lower limbic structures and is involved in higher-level human emotional processing, including empathy, planning, humor, and creativity, the health and development of these two circuits is critical for future self-regulation. When the toddler becomes a preschooler, she will be showing signs of some self-regulation as she attempts to inhibit her behavior herself.

New Skills

- She now walks well and can run, walk up and down stairs (she may need to hold on to the wall), jump, and walk sideways and backwards.

- She can stack a few blocks, use a pencil or crayon to copy a vertical line, and put a shaped block into its matching slot.

- She uses words to make her wishes known and can put two words together to form a short sentence.

- She knows most of the words for her clothing and can point, touch, or retrieve most clothing items.

- She loves to do what you do and wants to be just like you, so if you are putting on lipstick, she may want lipstick too.

- She can sing along with you and get many of the words and body movements correct. Her articulation of new words will not be as clear, but she will try to match your pronunciation when she hears it.

- She has learned the word "no" by now and uses it to make her wishes clear. She may be possessive of her toys.

- She can identify most of the characters in her familiar story-books and may insist that she turn the pages herself.

- She wants to try things herself and may push your arm away if you try to help her.

CULTIVATING SECURE ATTACHMENT IN THE EIGHTEEN-MONTH-OLD

Following your child's lead is now often interrupted as you take the lead to redirect, correct, or outright stop behavior. Parents will have made it easier on themselves if they started redirecting, substituting, and explaining feelings as soon as their child started to more freely move around. It is important to take the time to communicate a few reasons why you are stopping play, using a matter-of-fact tone, because your toddler understands more than she speaks. Using a matter-of-fact voice, a simple "I know you want to play, but it's time to go now. Would you like your blanket?" will go a long way. It is also important for you to identify your toddler's feelings. For example, when she gets very angry and kicks her toys, moving closer to her, looking her in the eyes while using a soft but firm voice, you can say, "I know you are frustrated that your toy won't work right now, but we don't kick toys. Let's see if we can get it fixed. In the meantime, let's play with the blocks." Or you can simply say, "Do you want to play with these blocks?" Or if she has fallen and is sobbing because it scared her, you may want to pick her up and hold her, saying, "That scared you, didn't it? You're okay." And then offer the Band-Aid cure! Band-Aids work magic, especially if you have the child variety, with colors and characters on them, to offer a choice.

Another magical word that helps keep the attachment bond present is "we." "We" means, of course, you and me, parent and child. It means "us," so it always brings the relationship to whatever situation you are working with and helps your child feel secure. And someday you may overhear your preschooler playing with another and saying with much assuredness, insistence, and confidence, "We don't do it that way!"

Morgan, Deborah, and Will: Healing Morgan's Attachment Wound

You can see by now just how much a secure attachment is needed to ride the rapids of the toddler stage. Parents are providing a new level of emotional regulation for their toddler's erupting and conflicting feelings, and this new level is based upon the secure history they have already built with their child. Dad now plays an incredibly important regulatory role by taking the heat off the mother-child relationship, where much of the drama is being played out. This period can be particularly difficult for single parents if they don't have the committed support of a family member or friend. Finally, you know that inhibition of behavior is a normal occurrence at this age and that it triggers the PNS. Again, in cases of hyperarousal without interactive regulation, the body itself will attempt to regulate this hyperaroused state by dramatically switching to PNS control for survival.

You may remember from chapter 1 that children hospitalized without their parents loudly protested the loss of their mother and that others could not soothe them. When the mother did not return, the child appeared to despair, and when the mother was finally reunited with her child, the child appeared detached as if she no longer cared about the mother. Upon further investigation, we found that Morgan had gone through a similar sequence of events when she went to live with her aunt; her aunt had interpreted the "quieting down" of her despair as her settling in to her new environment. However, when she returned home, her attachment to her mother was obviously changed. The ambivalence that is typical for this age was also amiss, as Morgan could no longer use her mother as a secure base for exploration. Instead, she tended to hang out on the periphery, watching her mother, which eventually made her mother uncomfortable. It would be quite scary for Morgan to explore much, since she felt she had no base to come back to. It is also likely that after experiencing the terror of losing her mother, playing might have felt scary to her. That is, during her mother's absence, Morgan's own body had regulated out of a hyperaroused state, and now the increased energy alone, which is needed for play, might have been too much for her to handle. All of this reinforced an inhibition for exploration, overemphasizing the PNS side of the nervous system. This profound entrainment of the nervous system more toward inhibition could have affected Morgan permanently if we couldn't help her feel safe again.

Deborah also reported that when she tried to cuddle with Morgan, the child pushed her away and preferred to be on her own. This made Deborah feel awful, sad, guilty, and eventually angry, setting up the beginning of a potentially intense cycle of preoccupation with each other, one that could be held in perpetuity if not corrected and that would never lead to true separation and individuation. There was also the concern that if Morgan could not begin to feel safe enough to play, thereby using her SNS for exploration, the avoidance of arousal could seal her off from the richness of play in general ... not a good trajectory. This all, of course, was an especially difficult situation when Morgan's father was not around much and her mother was still recovering.

In therapy, we made several immediate decisions. Because Deborah was a stay-at-home mom, I suggested that Morgan be taken out of child care until things settled down, as being away from her mother was contrary to what Morgan needed. I also requested that Will come in to a session when he returned. In several sessions with Deborah, she became aware of what Morgan's experience had been like. She talked with her sister now with a better eye to Morgan's emotions and confirmed that she had appeared to detach. We established household routines where Deborah was very consistent, including a nighttime routine that included reading to Morgan. Deborah was encouraged to nonverbally stroke Morgan's hair or give her a kiss if she showed any signs of resting on her body. Deborah was encouraged to have music time and dance with Morgan on a regular basis (thereby increasing SNS activity) and to take her to the park and beach to let her play. I also encouraged Deborah to talk with Morgan about how much she missed her when she was gone and, eventually, about how hard she knew it was for Morgan. I encouraged her to trust her own instincts about when the timing would be right. After many months of this approach, Deborah reported to me that during one of these "talks," Morgan collapsed onto her and fell asleep. Of course, we both cried. This was the first sign that healing was occurring in their bond.

When Will returned and saw the seriousness of what had happened, he made every effort not to work when he was home (at least not during the day while Morgan was awake) and tried as much as he could to shorten his travel. I asked Deborah and Will to put a good picture of the three of them on a coffee table in the living room, as well as in Morgan's own room, so that Morgan would be reminded of her father when he was gone. Will also changed his calling style. Instead of calling to make sure everything was okay, he now called and talked with Morgan about something he saw and then e-mailed a picture of it. Morgan loved this and put the pictures up in her room. Fortunately, too, Deborah's health improved. The marital relationship was also strengthened, and the family bond became more secure. After a year and a half of therapy, Morgan, now a preschooler, appeared to me to be developing in a more typical fashion. On the day I saw her last, she was happy and excited because she was soon to have a baby sister!

PLAY AND ATTACHMENT IN THE EIGHTEEN-MONTH-OLD

The eighteen-month-old needs your ongoing safety and security, even when she is moving away from you to explore and seems a bit more independent. Ongoing reassurance that she is okay, even when you need to stop worrisome behavior or when she initially tries and fails a task, helps make her life doable. She will want to know how to do things and will love special projects, like making a card for a sick neighbor. Helping her through the tough transitions of having to leave her play for bedtime, or worse, having to try to share, helps her develop new skills and independence from the trust and security of your relationship.

GAMES: Imitating and Naming

- Eighteen-month-olds love to do what you are doing, so if you are grocery shopping, using a big cart, your eighteen-month-old will like to follow along with her child cart. Don't be surprised if you turn around, and she has loaded her cart with items found on low shelves!

- Singing all kinds of simple songs with body movements is immensely fun. You will likely hear her humming these tunes in other places. You may find that she has unexpectedly created a new sound or word for an event or person.

- Asking her "where's your ..." questions will help her learn her body parts and the names of her personal belongings.

- Feeding the animals is always a fun game; planting seeds in the garden and watching them grow is great fun for an eighteen-month-old. She might also get very interested in something she sees, like a worm.

- Having a few big magnets on the lower part of your refrigerator so that your eighteen-month-old can hang her pictures will make her feel great about her art.

- When she says something like "doggie," asking her yes-and-no questions, like "is the doggie wagging his tail?" not only extends the conversation, but also shows her you are interested in what she says.

- Having dress-up clothes and shoes that are close to a full-length mirror helps her not only play and imitate grown-ups but also gives her different views of herself.

- Making toys is immensely fun for the young toddler. Stringing large beads to make a necklace will be very entertaining.

PARENT FOCUS: A SINGLE DAD AT PLAY

In San Diego, several male psychologists specialize in working with fathers and their young children. There's a Saturday morning support group for fathers who bring their young infants. There, fathers share time with other men and their babies and ask questions or talk about their relationship with their babies. Ed was one of those fathers who attended the group regularly and made friends with other fathers. Ed's relationship with his wife ended when his son Dustin was six months old, but Ed and Dustin's mother were doing the best they could to co-parent. Ed adored Dustin and was committed to keeping the boy's life stable. One of the fathers from the group invited Ed and Dustin to join his family on a picnic at a park. As the two men talked, a plan to have a volleyball tournament evolved. More people were invited to make teams, and soon they had a day at the park. The dads rotated game time with watching and playing with the children as the other dads played ball. Brilliant dads!

LIVING IN THE CHARM: OWEN'S LEARNING HOW TO COUNT

Eighteen-month-old Owen was learning to count. When asked to count, he would start, very seriously, "one, two, three, four, five, six, daddy, eight, nine, ten." It took another six months to find the number seven!

CHAPTER 10

Where Did He Hear That Word?

The Two-Year-Old

Brown Bear, Brown Bear, What do you see?
I see a red bird looking at me.
—Bill Martin Jr. and Eric Carle,
Brown Bear, Brown Bear, What Do You See?

If you want to find a word that describes the overall look of a two-year-old, it would have to be "busy." Two-year-olds virtually burst on any scene commanding the attention of all. Their curiosity is endless, and they want to experience and play with everything. Their previous nonverbal understanding of their world is now being filled in with words at a rate that matches no other time in life. The two-year-old is often learning ten to fifteen new words a week! Even though a two-year-old's pronunciation can be poor, parents might be surprised by their more advanced toddler's language acquisition. Imitating you has been going on for some time, but up to now, it has been more nonverbal. Now your more advanced toddler will repeat what he hears, leaving you to monitor what you say. As the two-year-old becomes more verbal, however, he often gives the impression that he is older than he really is. The two-year-old is still a young child who continues to have dramatic ups and downs in his emotions, including tantrums, so he still needs sensitive understanding and help from his parents to regulate these emotions. In fact, that familiarity with the word "no" at eighteen months has somehow advanced to a toddler with his hands on his hips, looking quite unabashedly into your eyes to say "no!"

Setting limits can be a challenge. Somewhere along the way, your cuddly, cooing infant exploded into a person who is everywhere at once! But setting limits during the toddler years actually guides behavior and teaches your toddler that though what he wants is important, there are other considerations that he has to begin learning. Although this can be tough, if he is throwing a fit because his needs are not being met "now," it actually makes him feel more secure that you insist on a standard for behavior; it also teaches him a lot about problem solving. Parents who have trouble setting limits during the toddler stage may find themselves overwhelmed by a preschooler who still wants his way and has not learned that other people have rights too. Although you will use the word "no" (and sometimes often), there are other ways to anticipate and redirect your toddler's strong emotions.

SETTING THE SCENE: COHEN'S STRUGGLE WITH HIS MOTHER

Cohen was a cute two-and-a-half-year-old boy whose left eye was significantly turned out (called *strabismus*). Cohen's pediatric ophthalmologist referred Cohen and his mother, Wanda, to me. On the phone before the appointment, Wanda said, "You have to help me, I can't handle this eye thing anymore." Wanda was referring to Cohen's reaction to his treatment to correct his eyes. His ophthalmologist had recommended that he have vision therapy, which Cohen didn't mind so much. He also recommended that Cohen wear an eye patch every day for up to two hours while Wanda helped him focus on "near" work. The patch would cover the good eye, which would hopefully strengthen the eye muscles in his weaker eye and correct his strabismus. If no treatment were given, Cohen's brain could favor taking in information with his good eye only, virtually shutting down input into his weak eye and affecting his focus and depth perception.

Wanda reported that she and Cohen were currently living with Wanda's sister to save on rent while Cohen's father, Bill, was away. Bill was working on a construction job in another state and was not expected back for several months. Wanda took classes at a junior college and hoped to have her associate's degree in marketing by the following year. The current concern was Cohen's reaction to the eye patch. Wanda reported that he "fights her" and had even kicked and bitten her when she tried to put the patch on. She also said that Bill "never handles any of his eye issues either because he always had a hard time looking at him." Several issues stood out:

1. Wanda was, in effect, raising Cohen herself without much help from Bill or her sister, who worked full time. She was also exasperated with Cohen's additional medical requirements.

2. Cohen was a two-year-old with normal two-year-old desires and conflicts who was confronted now with patching the only eye he saw well out of, leaving him with marginal vision at best to learn and explore.

3. Bill was not around to help take the edge off of this mother-toddler conflict.

The two-year-old will use his will to try to continue his play and exploration, which shows how compelling and primary play is to learning. He will fight to continue having his way if not provided a way to transition to another activity or task. Matter-of-fact parents who are sensitive to the reasons their toddler doesn't want to share his toys or go to bed or leave his play for dinner are in a better position to take creative approaches to getting their toddler to comply without losing their own emotional regulation. This is not an easy task sometimes, especially when changes in the home or new requirements arise, like Cohen's eye treatment, that have not been well established in safe routines. For Wanda and Cohen, the situation was further complicated by Wanda's own stress in trying to put the patch on Cohen as the doctor had ordered, for when she did, Cohen would become aggressive with Wanda. I will return to Cohen, Wanda, and Bill when I discuss secure attachment in two-year-olds, but first here's a look at typical physical, social-emotional, and brain development for this age group.

DEVELOPMENTAL MILESTONES: BUILDING CONNECTION AS YOUR TODDLER GROWS

As in all other developmental periods, your relationship with your child is primary and keeps your toddler feeling secure. Responding to his needs to play, explore, and learn while helping him regulate his negative emotions and changing them more toward positive outcomes is what builds confidence and security in your child. The two-year-old toddler's emotions continue to be immediate, and you may find him saying "I love you" and "I hate you" in the course of a single day. Accepting your toddler's feelings without feeling hurt yourself is often easier if you can say something back like "I know you are angry with Mommy because you can't go outside, but maybe we can blow some bubbles while you take your bath?" Chances are you will see a mood shift right away, and it's a nice compromise: he gets the bubbles and you get the bath!

Two-year-olds are very imaginative and like to pretend. They are also beginning to learn concepts: naming body parts, colors, numbers, shapes, and eventually letters, which builds their knowledge base in an orderly fashion and helps them prepare for school. There is no need to force this learning, however, as you will find that you can emphasize concepts using books that you read or games that you play together. Your toddler will be experiencing play but will also know you are proud of him when he gets the color or shape right. At this stage, you can also introduce the alphabet song. Here's a look at what the typically developing two-year-old can do. Remember that developmental ranges are wide, and the list below covers an entire year that is chock-full of growth. If you have any worries about your child's development, it's best to consult with your pediatrician.

Your Toddler's Physical and Social-Emotional Development

In general, the two-year-old can do the following:

- Run with coordination, swing his leg to kick a ball, and walk on his tiptoes.

- Name objects in books and pictures, put puzzle pieces in a simple puzzle, and build a tower with blocks.

- Match three to four colors, pick out one requested item from an array of items, and use pronouns like "I," "me," "you," "she," and "he."

- Use three-word sentences, pose questions, extend the conversation by offering additional details like saying the color of a truck that you pointed out. He also may be using past tense.

- Hold his paper with one hand or arm while he colors with his other hand. He may be able to draw a horizontal line.

- Understand the concept of "one" and compare sizes and weights.

- Understand a few prepositions, like "in," "under," or "between."

- Commonly want to do things himself and often tell you "I did it!"

- Like to imitate and do pretend play. Will play alongside another child but not interactively. May offer toys to other children but may suddenly also want them back.

- Be interested in dressing himself, brushing his teeth, and may be indicating an interest in toilet training.

- Be demanding, with strong emotions that change quickly. He can also have tantrums and show aggression when frustrated. He may try to be destructive with his toys. He can also develop fears.

Your Toddler's Brain Development

By the end of the second year, the structure of your toddler's brain is similar to the adult brain (Matsuzawa et al. 2001), although it will take a much longer time before it functions like an adult brain. The orbitofrontal cortex continues to mature, reaching the height of its critical developmental period by two and a half years (Schore 2001a). This structure, with its connections to lower limbic systems, will eventually allow your child to reflect on his own emotions. At this stage of development, however, the parent interprets the toddler's emotions and not only helps him understand what he is feeling but also helps name his feelings while actively working with him to regulate those feelings. This keeps his nervous system in a range that promotes growth, exploration, and development. As you know from chapter 2, a balance of emotions tipped more toward the positive releases the biochemicals associated with vitality, which feels good.

By naming his emotions and feelings for him (something he can't do yet), while helping him down-regulate high arousal or up-regulate low arousal, you make him feel secure. Since he knows that his parents can make him feel good, he can get on with playing, which is fun. For his future self-regulation, he is also learning how you did it. This change in regulation starts to be seen in the preschooler, and it has much to do with the combination of your ongoing sensitive-enough regulation of your toddler's emotions, your toddler's learning and exploration, and his imitation of what you do. In fact, there is some evidence that the ability to imitate is associated with better memory recall and sequencing of events, even at young ages (Lukowski et al. 2005). The upcoming sensitive period for left hemisphere development, beginning somewhere between two and a half and three years (Chiron et al. 1997), is on the horizon. This is why verbal language and language concepts are salient for the two-year-old.

New Skills

- He can feed himself, pick up a book to look at, fetch an article of clothing, and toss a ball.

- He can walk without help, run, and walk up and down stairs holding on to the wall or railing. He also may be able to ride a tricycle.

- He can identify the source of many sounds if you ask him "what's that?"

- He can participate in cleanup time by helping to pick up his toys.

- He can have conversations with himself while playing and can make his wishes known using two- to three-word sentences.

- He loves stories and songs, and you may hear him singing one of his favorite songs while he plays.

- He knows his body parts and is learning his numbers and shapes.

- He knows if he is a boy or a girl and can tell you his age.

- He gets easily frustrated and is possessive of his toys. He can be cooperative and affectionate too.

CULTIVATING SECURE ATTACHMENT IN THE TWO-YEAR-OLD

Just as soon as you think things are under control, something else happens. That's the story with two-year-olds. On one of my train trips to Los Angeles, two-year-old Adrienne was sitting on her mother's lap while her grandmother was sitting in the seat across the aisle. Two-year-olds like "me" conversations, so she was quite happy to answer her grandmother's question "Why don't you have your seat belt on?" with "Cause there's no buckle!" Exaggerated "why" games are always fun for toddlers (and preschoolers too), but instead of continuing the game, mother and grandmother began talking on their own. Adrienne then took a sip of water, held it in her mouth, slipped off her mother's lap, walked around to the seat in front of her, spit the water on her older sister who was seated there, and returned to her mother with a smug smile on her face. Of course, the sister lamented loudly that Adrienne had spit on her. Her mother then stated firmly, "We don't spit. Go apologize to your sister," which Adrienne did. But the big sister wouldn't accept Adrienne's apology, even with Adrienne pleading. Adrienne's mood now shifted to tears because her sister was "mean to her." Grandmother calmly said, "Maybe she will accept your apology in a few minutes. Why don't you sit on my lap?" Adrienne did, and her mother and grandmother continued their conversation. Brilliant mom and grandmother! This interaction, including the shifts in mood, took all of four minutes with these matter-of-fact adults.

What parents often are confronted with is that their toddler's emotions trigger their own emotions, causing the adult to be dysregulated. As you already know, routines are important in emotional regulation, as is the use of the word "we." Both will go a long way in helping your toddler (and you) through the day, as long as the routines are still fun, and "we" is not overly used, as the toddler, of course, is more interested in "me." Using a calm, matter-of-fact voice will help move everyone through unexpected emotional states and will move your toddler along.

Another parent skill that helps life run smoothly is announcing a transition before it happens. For the two-year-old, providing transitions helps him see what the next step is, thereby enhancing his ability to let go of what he is doing now. Also, mentioning something interesting about what he will be doing next helps to move him along without too much fuss. For example, the mother of two-year-old Nick said, "Nick, it's time to put your toys away because dinner is ready." Now, unless a toddler smells his favorite food or is starving, dinner is generally not a compelling reason to stop playing with toys. But then Nick's mother added, "I've made your favorite, macaroni and cheese. Do you want to put out the placemats?" Now we're talking!

Cohen, Wanda, and Bill: Creating a Healing Routine

Toddlers, of course, are generally easily frustrated. They like to play a lot, and they like to try things on their own. Regulating a toddler's emotions is a hard task for any parent during this stage. For Wanda, this was exponentially true because she had the odious task of "blinding" her son once a day so that his weak eye could become stronger, and she was doing this without support from Bill. As we began to establish a starting point, Wanda revealed that she dreaded these interactions with Cohen, and she feared that they were affecting her feelings for him. She found herself avoiding the patch and only trying again when she couldn't stand the guilt. She admitted that no "near work" had been done to date because Cohen was too upset. A different approach was needed, and I asked Wanda to sign releases so that I could coordinate Cohen's treatment with his ophthalmologist and vision therapist.

It became clear that Wanda had no routine for putting the eye patch on Cohen, who likely experienced her as coming out of nowhere to take his vision away. He seemed to respond to her with a fight-or-flight response that comes from the amygdala's appraisal of the situation. Since Cohen experienced his mother differently before patching, this change in her behavior would not only have been extremely frightening but also incredibly disorganizing to him, especially when he was also likely experiencing for the first time the differences in his two eyes. Until now, Cohen really didn't experience a problem with his eyes (although he may have received conflicting messages from his father, if Bill did have trouble looking at him), but now with the patching, his wonderfully exciting visual world disappeared or became blurry and gray. Now that's scary.

Wanda and Cohen sat on the floor in my office in front of a large stuffed giraffe, and with coaching, Wanda began to talk to Cohen about his eyes. She explained to him that although he had two perfectly good eyes, one of his eyes didn't see as well as the other because it needed "stronger muscles" and that's why he was going to visit his doctors. I encouraged Wanda to let Cohen leave at any point during the conversation if he wanted to play with toys in the corner, and that she should just comment, "You want to play now." Cohen did go over to the toys, but soon he returned, and Wanda continued talking to him about his eyes. With much sensitivity, Wanda explained that putting the patch on his good eye helped his other eye build muscles "like a muscleman" and that the doctor said that if he can build big muscles in his eye, he would be able to see many more things. We started with having Cohen put the patch on the giraffe, so he could see how it looked. With some help, we created a doctor-approved plan for Wanda and Cohen to start "building his muscles" every day before lunch for a half hour. This would be followed by lunch and a quiet time when Wanda read him a book.

Wanda explained to Cohen that during the "muscle-building time," she would put the patch on his right eye but that he could pick out one of his stickers first and put it on the patch. After that, they would play a game together until the bell went off on the kitchen timer (which he could hear ticking). One of the games we designed was using a big "I Spy" book, where Cohen could try to find an object in an array of objects. Another was reaching his hand in a bag, picking up one of several objects inside, and saying what it was. Wanda was to then ask him a question about the object that required vision, like the color of the object. A third game was inventing a story together, with Wanda starting out by saying "once upon a time" and then drawing a picture of the story. And a fourth game was a memory game, flipping over cards turned facedown on a tabletop. Wanda was advised not to put the patch on if he didn't pick out the sticker, as we wanted him to participate in the treatment, not be a victim of it, and to simply put the "I Spy" book and the sticker sheet on the table. If he didn't pick out a sticker, Wanda was also advised to take the book and stickers up after ten minutes and simply say, "We can try again tomorrow." Within two weeks, Cohen was playing the games with his mother, who never again tried to put the patch on him without the consenting sticker. Although effort was made to have Bill become a part of the treatment, he declined to participate.

PLAY AND ATTACHMENT IN THE TWO-YEAR-OLD

Two-year-olds want to try things themselves; you can continue to support your secure relationship by encouraging their exploration and problem solving and helping out when things don't go as expected. Giving two choices now not only supports independence, but you can guide your toddler by offering choices that are acceptable to both of you: "Do you want to wear your green shirt or your new Spider-Man shirt?" Toddlers won't want to share, but they still need to hear how you handle it. So a toddler who has just grabbed "his" toy from his baby brother, who is now crying, can be approached with, "I know you wanted your toy back, but Doug was playing with it when you grabbed it from him. You can let him play with it for a few minutes while you play with something else, or you can give him another toy to play with." This is helping the toddler learn how to solve problems, and it will lead to avoiding future conflict as the toddler learns to solve problems himself.

GAMES: Making Things and Problem Solving

- Two-year-olds enjoy coloring or putting stickers on a bookmark.

- Your two-year-old will like it if you fill a paper bag with objects that feel different and then ask him to pull out something that is "hard," "soft," or "rough."

- He will enjoy making a giant picture of himself. You can cut off a big sheet of butcher paper and have your toddler lay down on it. Carefully trace the entire outline of your toddler's body and then have him color in his clothes and face.

- He likes playing matching color games and will like it if you ask him to find all the "red" things he sees in the room.

- Hiding games that stress hiding an object "under," "between," or "on top" of something can be a lot of fun for him, especially if he shuts his eyes while you hide the object.

- Expanding conversations with your toddler by adding a few more details to what he is doing will help him do the same.

- Tossing or kicking a ball with him is also a fun game for him.

- Going to the park and playing on the swings, climbing the slides, and riding his tricycle is fabulous for your toddler. You will need to stay close by, though, as he will need help.

PARENT FOCUS: A DAY AT THE SPA

One of the nicest stories I've heard about staying sane during the toddler period came from Joe and Jeralina. Joe surprised Jeralina with a two-day trip to a high-end spa where she was pampered at every moment. She, in turn, surprised him with a party with all their friends and family to celebrate "what a wonderful husband I have." Now this is good!

It's important to take care of yourself and your partner, especially during the toddler years, when it's so easy to burn out. When parents see to their own needs while taking care of their toddler, their child learns that he is a part of a family that contains other important relationships. This helps him expand his "me" focus, if reluctantly, to include others. This implicit experience of how relationships work eventually turns into the knowledge that he doesn't need to worry about his parents; they can take care of both themselves and him. This is security.

LIVING IN THE CHARM: TESS'S PUSH BACK

Nathan and Heather Easley had two young children: two-year-old Tess and four-year-old Peter. One afternoon while Tess and Peter were playing together, Heather heard a loud unhappy scream from Tess. She went over to see what the commotion was about. As soon as Tess saw her mother, she said, "Pete Easley did it. Pete Easley did it."

CHAPTER 11

Shifting to the Left:
The Three-Year-Old

*If you give a mouse a cookie, he's going to
ask for a glass of milk. When you give him
the milk, he'll probably ask you for a straw.*
—Laura Joffe Numeroff,
If You Give a Mouse a Cookie

Having proceeded step-by-step through the developmental stages during
the first three years of life, you should not be surprised by how your
child's internal working model of relationships grew out of your own
dyadic, lived experience with her. All of her experience with you has
formed what Daniel Stern (1985) calls *representations of interactions that
have been generalized*, or RIGs, that are now embedded into the implicit
memory structures deep within her brain. She now has a "feels right"
system of relating that will guide her own behavior and help her regulate
her own emotions based upon her experience with you. I was recently
at a talk given by another professional who works with infants. She said
that if she had known about how important affect regulation and its
outcome were on development, she wonders if she would have had the

courage to raise her children. This is understandable, especially if we slip into our left brains and think about what we are doing! Fortunately, the young child is right-brained, helping us to find, refind, or simply luxuriate back into right-brain-to-right-brain conversations, and that is the charm of childhood.

The three-year-old is starting to move into a left hemisphere growth period (Chiron et al. 1997), where the structure of language development leads to the astonishing abilities of abstract thought. When this stage is sitting on a solidly constructed right hemisphere within an entrained autonomic nervous system, one that has been regulated by attuned and sensitive parents, you will have given your child the human qualities of empathy, creativity, insight, planning, motivation, initiation, and humor. More importantly, her knowledge of who she is, that is, her sense of self, grows from her experience that she is cared for by her parents, who have understood her feelings, helped her feel better, and helped her solve the problems she has encountered. Secure and confident, she now enters the world of the preschooler. What an accomplishment!

SETTING THE SCENE: KIERRA'S WORKING FOR ATTENTION

Three-year-old Kierra came in for her first family session with her mother and stepfather. Ester and Victor had met when Kierra was two years old; they had married six months later. In an earlier meeting with Ester and Victor, Ester had said that Kierra wasn't adjusting well to having a stepfather and seemed to now want to be with her biological father, Ed, more. Ester felt confused by this, but because she didn't want to deprive Kierra of her father, she had arranged a number of prolonged visits with him. Upon returning home to Ester and Victor after these visits, Kierra had been hard to live with. She was bossy, defiant, and often mean to her mother. Victor tried to step in to discipline Kierra, only to find that Ester would "attack" him. Victor also felt that Kierra always wanted Ester's attention and would try to "deliberately" exclude him. In the beginning, he felt it was just because she was getting used to him, but now he believed it was getting out of control.

On further interview, Ester stated that though her pregnancy and Kierra's birth had been normal, her relationship with Kierra's father had started to deteriorate as soon as Kierra was born. Ester said that it was the hardest time in her life as she tried to take care of Kierra as her marriage was falling apart. She admitted to being seriously depressed until Victor came into her life. She said that her relationship with Kierra's father had improved "somewhat" since the divorce, but there was still tension between them over Kierra's care. They shared joint custody of Kierra, who was spending half of her week with each parent. Kierra had been in child care since she was twelve months old, when Ester had started working. Both Ester and Victor reported that the bossiness at home was also seen in child care, and there had been several reports of incidents where Kierra had pulled another girl's hair, scattered or thrown toys, and refused to clean up.

When I met Kierra, I found her to be a cute three-year-old with a strong presence. While we were all talking together, Kierra tried to stop the conversation by forcefully pulling on her mother's clothes and repeating "Mommy" a number of times. She eventually used a very loud voice, prompting Ester to turn to her in frustration and ask, "What do you want, Kierra?" Kierra then began pulling her mother toward the toy corner to show her some toys. Ester got up to go with her, briefly looked at a few toys, and then encouraged Kierra to play while "Mommy and Victor talk." Kierra promptly took the bucket of Legos over to her mother and dumped all of them out by her feet, saying, "I want to build a house." Several issues stood out:

1. Ester appeared quite ambivalent about her relationship with Kierra and especially about her seeing her father, a man she had acrimonious feelings toward. She also seemed to want to please both Kierra and Victor but expressed no sense of her own point of view.

2. Victor appeared confused about his fathering role and looked to Ester for support. He was especially upset and confused when he tried to discipline a disrespectful child, only to have his wife get angry with him. He also showed no signs of playing with Kierra or interacting positively with her.

3. Kierra appeared to be actually working hard for her mother's attention. She did appear to completely ignore Victor.

The three-year-old loves conversation and will ask you many questions. They also love to help out in the house because it makes them feel they are part of the family. Three-year-olds are also astute observers and will generally talk about what they see. I suspected that other issues besides her stepfather were involved in Kierra's negativity and controlling behavior. What was immediately obvious was that there were no conversations with her, no time for questions. I wasn't sure at this point if there were any routines at home in which Kierra could help out and feel a part of the family. In the session, Victor did not play or interact positively with Kierra, which, if representative of their home life together, would mean that Victor would have been trying to discipline a child he had no relationship with! Never a good idea. I will return to Kierra, Ester, Victor, and Ed when I discuss secure attachment in three-year-olds, but first here's a look at typical physical, social-emotional, and brain development for this age group.

DEVELOPMENTAL MILESTONES: BUILDING CONNECTION AS YOUR PRESCHOOLER GROWS

Three-year-olds like to talk and are generally quite social within the family. They are very inquisitive and are combining their improved language skills with what they observe, resulting in the many questions commonly heard from a preschooler. They sound more grown up because their language is understandable, and they are using anywhere from three- to eight-word sentences. They will surprise you with adorable questions or answers that show you how they think. Remember three-year-old Pippa's thoughts about her new cousin Ingo in chapter 4? Three-year-olds also understand basic time concepts, like now versus later, and have developed spatial perspective of another's viewpoint. For example, if you sit a medium-sized box on a table and then give your three-year-old a small toy and ask her to use the box to hide the toy so you can't see it, she will put the toy on her side, out of your sight. If you now put a doll in a chair next to the table and ask the three-year-old to hide the toy so the doll can't see it, she will move the toy to the side of the box that's out of the doll's view. You may begin to feel less emotional turmoil in your three-year-old, who now wants to help out, likes your house rules (most of the time), and works to make you laugh. Even though she may appear so grown up, compared with the toddler, a three-year-old can still have her feelings hurt, be cranky when tired, show frustration when she can't make something work, and will still have trouble sharing.

Your Preschooler's Physical and Social-Emotional Development

In general, the three-year-old can do the following:

- Exhibit tremendous growth. She is likely taller and slimmer, and has a full set of baby teeth.

- Dress herself but may need help with front and back and may need help with buttons. She can brush her teeth with supervision and put on shoes (maybe backwards at first) but cannot tie shoelaces.

- Be potty-trained, although boys sometimes need a little longer.

- Use full sentences. Most of her speech is understandable, but she can still have some problems with pronunciation.

- Tell you a story and ask who, what, where, and why questions. She also likes you to read or retell her favorite stories word for word.

- Use a tricycle, climb a slide, and walk up and down steps alternating her feet.

- Draw a circle and may try to make a square, match objects with pictures, identify colors, count with one-to-one correspondence, and sort and classify objects.

- Build with blocks, put simple puzzles together, and combine toys to make a story, like shopping at a store or making a house.

- Understand time differences in words like "yesterday," "today," and "tomorrow" or "now" and "later."

- Know her gender and correctly tell you whether she will grow up to be a man or a woman.

- Enjoy helping out around the house and playing with other children for a short time.

Your Preschooler's Brain Development

The complexity of synaptic patterns and connections has greatly increased by three years of age, and the major fiber tracks can be identified in a three-year-old's brain (Matsuzawa et al. 2001). Your preschooler's brain also weighs about 80 percent of an adult brain (Trevarthen 1990). Through the coordinated processes of neuronal growth and pruning, your three-year-old's brain has been sculpted in response to her unique environment. Within a secure dyadic relationship, the limbic system is maturing with its subcortical-to-cortical circuitry in place. These important connections mean that the higher regulatory center (right orbitofrontal cortex) can override the lower centers (anterior cingulate and amygdala), allowing for future emotional self-regulation and a host of higher human capabilities (Schore 1994). A pattern of experience in relationships has been wired into implicit memory, giving the preschooler a foundation to stand on as she moves into the development of language.

A cycle of left hemisphere activation began when your preschooler was eighteen months old (Thatcher 1997), corresponding with the initial burst of language. However, by three years, the left hemisphere is entering a growth period (Chiron et al. 1997), allowing for increasing complexity in verbal communication. The cyclical movement between the hemispheres, however, will continue, as this process is thought to be involved in the organization and reorganization of brain systems as your child develops (Thatcher 1997).

The corpus callosum, which connects and transfers information between the two hemispheres, and the long connecting association fibers within each hemisphere are also developing, but these connections will continue to develop for some time (Trevarthen 1990). As the corpus callosum matures, some connections between right and left brain appear to be quicker to develop than others; the ability to identify objects by sight, for example, comes more quickly than the ability to identify them by touch. In one study, three-year-olds made many more cross-hemisphere errors (meaning the information didn't transfer well) than five-year-olds did when given a tactile fabric identification task (Galin et al. 1979).

New Skills

- She can dress herself with help, brush her teeth, and put on her shoes if you tie the laces.

- She can sing simple songs, ride a tricycle, and climb up and down on a slide.

- She understands "yesterday," "today," and "tomorrow," and "now" and "soon," but still may have a hard time waiting for "soon"!

- She can play with other children briefly but still has trouble sharing.

- She can sort by color and can sort knives, forks, and spoons.

- She can put a simple puzzle together, match and name colors, and match an object with a picture.

- She can make choices between two suggestions or objects.

- She is able to tell you a simple story.

- She is immensely curious about "who," "what," "where," "when," and especially "why."

CULTIVATING SECURE ATTACHMENT IN THE THREE-YEAR-OLD

Three-year-olds really want to help, and life goes better if you let them help in some way. This is the time when having your three-year-old contribute to the care of the house and home will make her feel a part of the family and very grown up. Three-year-olds like to know what to expect next and still need their routines. The maturing three-year-old will be comfortable having some time away from home. For children with a stay-at-home parent, they often do very well in a preschool class at this age. For those who have been in child care, going to the preschool room can be exciting and feel grown up. Three-year-olds also need choices, and giving them a choice between two items makes them feel more independent. They are also talkers who ask a lot of questions. Your three-year-old might ask you, "Why are you sewing a shirt?" "Because your brother ripped it." "Why did he rip it?" "Because he slid into base." "Why did he slide?" And so on, until you get enough consciousness to redirect her! Three-year-olds also have much improved motor coordination and can ride a tricycle with vigor. They can also draw, play with play dough, put together puzzles, throw balls, tell stories, and identify colors, animals, and body parts easily, and they have increased attention as they play.

Kierra, Ester, and Victor: Reducing Two Worlds to One

The natural movement of development is toward increasing complexity, so the older the child is, the more you need to identify the ingredients that went into the cake, so to speak. It is quite impossible to figure out what to do with any hope of making a change unless you have a basic understanding of the child's lived experience. The person with the most ongoing lived experience with Kierra was her mother. Ed, too, had ongoing lived experience with Kierra, and that relationship was also assessed in collateral sessions, but let's return to Ester.

Ester reported that she had been depressed after Kierra was born and that her depression was ongoing until she had met Victor. The effect of maternal depression on an infant is profound, with multiple studies showing increased negativity and emotional dysregulation in infants with depressed mothers (Murray and Cooper 1997). In fact, the infant researcher Tiffany Field found that newborns of mothers who were depressed in pregnancy were born with similar depression biochemistries, which resulted in a functionally depressed infant at birth (Field et al. 2004). Kierra's infancy was spent interacting with a depressed mother, who likely had trouble stimulating Kierra into the excitement of play states and who also likely had depressed facial expressions, voice, and gestures. Kierra may have learned more about negativity than about positive emotions during her first year of life. To add to this, Ester acknowledged that she and Ed would fight constantly, which could have easily exposed Kierra to stressed, dysregulated emotional states. When Kierra was one year old, her parents divorced, her father left the home, her mother went to work, and she went into child care and began living in two homes. At two, a new man came into her mother's home. This is a lot for a young child, but it also mirrors what happens in many lives. The key is how to provide a constant enough environment that is understandable to the child, all while supporting the child's particular stage of development. This is also a lot for parents to manage.

Often when families are blending in new people and realigning former relationships, the key people are focused more on the relationship boundaries in the former relationship (that will continue unless adjusted) than the new ones that need to form. You will remember that Morris in chapter 5 had trouble realigning the relationship boundaries that were established in his first marriage. Following a difficult marriage that ends in divorce, adults who are still trying to provide security for their children also may find life difficult. Now when the adult meets a new partner and falls in love, he or she is generally happy. Believe it or not, happiness in a parent that's the result of a new partner can be quite troublesome for the child who goes through this transition.

For Kierra, having her mother be happy with someone outside of her own relationship with her would have been hard, and it was understandable that Kierra wanted to be with her father more, for with him, she only experienced one relationship, her dad and hers. Do you see how different the world can look if you take the child's point of view? From Ester's point of view, Ester was finally with someone she felt happy with and with whom she felt she could make a home for Kierra. She could, but it wouldn't be a snap. I worked together with this family, including having several collateral visits with Ed and Kierra, focusing on the adults' understanding of Kierra's experienced world. We explored how Kierra likely developed negativity from the first year when Ester was so depressed and how her controlling behavior stemmed from her need for her mother's focused, sensitive, and reliable attention. Now that Ester had increased positive mood herself, though, and all adults were committed to trying to help Kierra, it appeared possible to make a change.

The first step was to talk with Kierra about.what had happened. Too often, adults do not talk to children about what is happening in their collective lives, so the children have no base from which to understand and handle their feelings. In therapy, Ester talked with Kierra about how her parents were good parents and both loved her, but they were not happy together and that's why "Mommy was always sad." She went on to say that she was glad that she'd met and married Victor because "Mommy feels happy now," and "we will make a happy family here with Victor, just like you have a happy family with Dad." One world. Victor was encouraged to use much sensitivity in building a relationship with Kierra of his own, and if he felt like "discipline" was needed, to use redirection. I encouraged both Victor and Ester to use excitement and anticipation to increase Kierra's vitality, set household routines where Kierra could help out, give her choices, read to her at night, at first with Ester, then with Ester and Victor, and finally with Victor, once the routine was established. Victor set up a swing set for Kierra in their backyard and offered Kierra pushes on the swing. Ester and Victor were encouraged to respond to Kierra when she approached them, look her in the eyes with sensitivity and affection, all while using a calm voice. They were also encouraged to have lots of conversations with her and to consider it a good sign whenever she asked a question. When Kierra used a controlling behavior or voice or when she whined, they began to use a matter-of-fact voice, telling her "that's not how we talk, so tell me again in your grown-up voice." As we went along, the newly forming family did more things together with Kierra, increasing her excitement and vitality. To his credit, Ed was able to see how his relationship with Ester had affected Kierra and did make some attempts to communicate with Ester in a more positive way. This was a long therapy that continues with check-ins to this day. Kierra's behavior has significantly changed as she has become more secure. She is in kindergarten at the time I am writing this and likes to be the teacher's helper.

PLAY AND ATTACHMENT IN THE THREE-YEAR-OLD

Three-year-olds like and need conversation, even if their questions drive you around the bend! They can play with other children for a while and may be starting to have playdates. They love stories about their parents and like particularly to hear stories about when they were a baby. They like to help out, although this goes better if you use questions, like "do you want to help Mommy make cookies?" They feel very grown up if you give them choices. Three-year-olds have more skills and will want to show you what they can do. Many three-year-olds like to play house, but remember they will imitate what they have seen in the home. Three-year-old Deborah loved to play house, and she had a mini–kitchen set and a child-sized table and chairs. One day, her eighteen-month-old brother wandered in. Deborah immediately snatched him, saying, "Sit here while I make eggs," and handed him the newspaper. Her mother, who caught this interaction, looked at her husband and said, "You make breakfast!"

GAMES: Conversations and Helping Out

• Three-year-olds like conversation and love to ask questions. Going through their baby book and talking about how they were as infants is wonderful for this age.

• Talking with your three-year-old about your own upbringing (even if it is a walking-to-school-in-five-feet-of-snow story!) gives her the security of her own family history.

• Memory games will continue to be fun for your three-year-old.

• She will enjoy making cards for someone who is sick, and she also feels good about helping someone else.

• Playing house is wonderful for both girls and boys.

• Playing with other children for a short time can also be fun, but she will still need help with sharing.

• Being with her family for a special outing is a lot of fun, especially if you talk about it and she can look forward to it.

• Giving her choices about what she likes or wants makes her feel very grown up: "You have to have a sweater to go out because it's cold. Do you want to wear your blue sweater or your brown sweater?"

PARENT FOCUS: FLOOR TIME FOR DAD

Oliver was a hardworking father of two children under the age of five. He tended to need some transition time when he came in from work before joining the family (see chapter 3 for more discussion of transition time). His wife, Laura, was also hardworking and exhausted when she got home. Both knew their children needed to be with them, since the kids had been in child care all day. Generally, they alternated picking up the kids with starting dinner. One day on Oliver's pickup day, he was in the bedroom changing his clothes and, for some reason, decided to get down on the floor. Within seconds, both children were on him, and when Laura came home, she found Oliver asleep on the floor with her four-year-old leaning up against him and "reading" a book to the two-year-old. It was such a sweet scene that Laura got down on the floor with them. Not joining in on a sweet scene because you are more driven by the next step (in this case, fixing dinner) means you miss out on emotional fill-ups!

LIVING IN THE CHARM: VALERIE'S PERPLEXITY

Ron and Leslie brought home their newborn son, Joseph, and laid him in the middle of their bed so that three-year-old Valerie could see her new brother. Valerie took a good look at him and then asked her mother, "Who is going to be that baby's mommy?"

CHAPTER 12

I Can Do It Myself:

The Four-Year-Old

How does a dinosaur clean up his room? With a
big bucketloader, or shovel, or broom? Does he
stick all his teddy bears under his bed, or shove
them all into his closet instead?
—Jane Yolen and Mark Teague,
How Do Dinosaurs Clean Their Rooms?

Four-year-olds love to tell jokes and will laugh hilariously even if you don't think it is funny. They also find great pleasure in repeating the joke just for the laugh. Four-year-olds are generally quite animated and can have intense emotions, including jealousy. You may find your four-year-old angry with you for giving his playmate attention. Four-year-olds speak using complex sentences, and their bursting thinking skills make for an interesting time for all. They can also complain if things aren't right and will easily tattle. Four-year-olds have very creative imaginations, and their play is now more symbolic. They will play out elaborate scenes, like running a grocery store or crossing an ocean in a boat. Playing with other children is fun, and four-year-olds will recruit other children into their play. They can generally take turns (sometimes with a reminder) and share, but they will change the rules of games to suit themselves. Four-year-olds can be very boastful and enjoy showing off what they can do. They still like to talk a lot and "why" is still the word of choice. Four-year-olds can also tell tall tales and may lie to avoid getting into trouble. They understand the concept of lying, however, so parents of four-year-olds can often avoid big scenes by simply asking their four-year-old if this is a true story or a pretend story. The four-year-old is in his last year of preschool, and it can be a poignant time for parents, who often feel this is the last of the childhood years (unless, of course, you have another one coming along). Before you know it, your child will be five and entering the new world of school-age children.

SETTING THE SCENE: DENNIS'S NEED FOR UNSTRUCTURED TIME

Dennis's parents, Myla and Bruce, called me for a consultation at the recommendation of a friend, because their only son, Dennis, had a hard time interacting with children on playdates. They reported that he always wanted an adult to stay with him. Dennis had a nanny, and if he went to someone else's house to play in the afternoons after preschool, he would insist that his nanny come with him and play along. When other kids came to his house, he insisted that she play with them there, too. Both Myla and Bruce worked full time, and they wanted a consultation to find out if Dennis's behavior was normal.

At the consultation, Dennis came in and sat between his parents. He was a cute four-year-old who was very quiet. His facial expressions were strikingly subdued, leaving me with the impression that Dennis was depressed. Contrary to the myth that the young child is too undeveloped to be depressed, young children can be depressed, and their faces and behavior can show it. Instead of going to the toy corner, Dennis stayed on the sofa. When he eventually talked, I could hear that his speech was good but soft.

Sometimes when working with families, starting a behavior change right away helps identify the issues, so I asked Dennis if he would like to do an "experiment" with his parents this week and come back and tell me if it worked. He gave a nod, so we designed a plan whereby at his next playdate at his house, he would play with his friend while the nanny did other things. Then both parents would come home, all of them would get in the car to take the playmate home, and then the family would go to the park together. There was a brief glint in Dennis's eye, which I read as "that might work."

His parents, however, immediately moved into an adult conversation about their schedules and how they could arrange being home at the same time. Both pulled out their electronic calendars and became absorbed in this to the point where it seemed they were no longer aware that anyone else was in the room. To my surprise, Dennis's father began talking with him about how hard this would be to arrange but that Dennis was "worth it." He said, "Daddy and Mommy are going to try very hard" to help him overcome his problem. Myla then joined in and said he was not to worry, though, for they "could make it happen." Then Myla moved to the floor and was now talking with Dennis (who was still on the sofa), using a quiet, intimate voice that had some pleading in it: "You could even decide what to bring with us to the park and what you would like to eat. Just tell me, I'll get it for you. Do you know? Can you think of anything?" Dennis was silent. Several concerns stood out:

1. Myla and Bruce interacted with Dennis in trying to solve a problem as if he were a colleague. Both were work absorbed and verbalized their inner thought processes so that Dennis heard way too much information, some of which must have been quite demoralizing for him to hear.

2. Dennis had no space to react, to be a typical four-year-old with four-year-old interests.

Though four-year-olds have increased language ability, they are nevertheless young children who need to play, joke around, show off their accomplishments, and have elaborate conversations with their parents. In this case, Dennis's parents were having elaborate conversations with him! I will return to Dennis, Myla, and Bruce when I discuss secure attachment in four-year-olds, but first here's a look at typical physical, social-emotional, and brain development for this age group.

DEVELOPMENTAL MILESTONES: BUILDING CONNECTION AS YOUR PRESCHOOLER GROWS

Four-year-olds like to do things their way and, more often than not, your four-year-old will insist that he do it himself. This takes more time (and finesse if you don't have the time) to move him along without too much fuss. Four-year-olds also like to test the limits of rules and can repeatedly ask you "why." Their language flexibility is remarkable, as they can now tell a younger sibling what is occurring using the younger sibling's language: "We're going 'bye-bye' now, Jackie." Four-year-olds have a much longer attention span than three-year-olds and can work on their activities until they feel like they're done. They can also use the telephone and talk to a relative for a short time. Four-year-olds can ask life-and-death questions, especially if someone in the family has died or a baby is born. If you are pregnant with another child, your four-year-old may want to know more about how that baby really did get in there! A response is always needed, but generally a simple answer like "Mommy has a special place in her where babies grow" will stave off the next series of questions for at least a while.

Your Preschooler's Physical and Social-Emotional Development

In general, the four-year-old can do the following:

- Run, jump, and skip with ease, and catch and throw balls

- Speak in complex sentences, know differences between small and large, heavy and light, and sort objects based upon these principles. He can also ask and answer questions.

- Recognize some letters and may be practicing printing his own name.

- Know his full name and may be learning his address and phone number.

- Name the primary colors and at least three shapes, count from one to six or seven objects, and follow a two-part instruction: "Please put your toys in the toy box and wash your hands for dinner."

- Put together a twelve- to fifteen-piece puzzle and form objects out of clay.

- Like to play with a few friends and may have identified one favorite friend. He is able to take turns and share for most of the time.

- Love dramatic play and to play out complex scenes, like working at a fire station, especially if he has just seen a fire station or visited one in the past.

- Feel intense emotions like jealousy and anger and can still have a meltdown if frustrated.

- Like to tell big, creative stories and may exaggerate. He can also lie to avoid your anger or consequences.

- Love to tell and retell jokes and will laugh hilariously, even if the jokes don't make sense to you.

Your Preschooler's Brain Development

An increasing complexity and organization is occurring in the four-year-old's brain that will continue for many years. Representations of the world are encoded into explicit memory, giving your preschooler increased memory capacity, so he can tell you what he did yesterday, for example. Cortical growth cycles will continue to occur throughout life, but at about four years, the left hemisphere appears to be integrating subsystems while the right hemisphere further differentiates what has already been integrated (Thatcher 1994, 1997). Neural networks involved in the right orbitofrontal cortex continue to develop, allowing for improved attention skills and emotional regulation (Schore 1994). However, four-year-olds are not yet able to perform many of the more

195

complex activities associated with frontal lobe processing, such as planning and solving complex problems (Luciana and Nelson 1998). It will also take another six to eight years for the corpus callosum to mature, allowing for the rapid transfer of information from one hemisphere to the other (Trevarthen 1990). In fact, one study investigating the interhemispheric transfer in four-, seven-, and ten-year-olds found that four-year-olds had the greatest number of errors, indicating incomplete transfer between the hemispheres (Joseph et al. 1984). The researchers also found that the four-year-olds appeared undaunted by the task, as they would just make up their own story about what was presented!

New Skills

- He can speak in complex sentences that include time sequences: "It fell off the table before I could grab it."

- He knows the difference between smallest and largest and can bring you the smallest crayon if you ask.

- He knows many simple songs and may sing them while he moves around the house.

- He is able to run, jump, skip, hop on one foot, catch and throw balls, and skillfully use a fork, spoon, and dinner knife.

- When speaking to a younger child, he will adjust his language to their level of understanding: "Mommy's getting 'ba-ba.'"

- He likes playing with other children and can take turns and share much of the time.

- He loves conversations and can tell elaborate stories. He can also ask and answer "who," "what," "where," "when," and "why" questions.

- He can be fearful of the dark and may worry about "monsters."

- He likes to tell jokes and can use a "bad word" (that he knows he's not supposed to use) just to see what will happen.

CULTIVATING SECURE ATTACHMENT IN THE FOUR-YEAR-OLD

Four-year-olds are generally full of energy, and they love conversation. They can tell silly jokes and then laugh hilariously. In fact, an odd-sounding word or a rhyming combination of a silly sound can cause four-year-olds to laugh hysterically, thereby prompting them to repeat the sounds many times over, until an adult says, "All right, already!" Four-year-olds also like to play with other children and, for the most part, can take turns and share. Their play with other children can go well, especially if there is an adult or parent moving around in the background to help them when they need help. Four-year-olds engage in imaginative play and like to show off what they know. Dennis was not displaying most of these qualities. Now that you know more about what a typically developing four-year-old looks like, let's take another look at Dennis, Myla, and Bruce.

Dennis, Myla, and Bruce: Making Room for Play

Myla and Bruce appeared to me to be left-brained people. By this, I mean that they were very structured, verbal, and had a hard time playing themselves. They were, of course, being themselves with Dennis, who was showing signs of depression and insecurity. As you well know by now, infants, toddlers, and preschoolers are more right-brained, and it is only at around two and a half to three years of age that the left hemisphere begins to come online, shifting the focus of development more toward the use of verbal language. Hopefully, when this shift occurs, the right hemisphere is rich in fibers that have fully connected all of its systems, particularly the subcortical-to-cortical tracks. Again, this occurs as sensitive parents amplify their child's arousal levels through play states while regulating his negative emotions, all while supporting the tasks within each stage of development.

Children who have not had sufficient right-brain-to-right-brain attunement are at a disadvantage as development shifts to the left hemisphere. Emotional regulation problems can be seen in preschoolers, and if the problem is severe enough, it can affect what the child is able to learn. Think of it this way: if you felt unsafe, would you reach for a math book? Generally, fear scrambles our brains, so to speak, making it difficult to focus, let alone play or learn. Dennis was showing us that basically he was too scared to play, and a close history of his first three years confirmed an extremely structured home where play was never spontaneous. Since we are who we are, Dennis's parents had to learn to see how the lack of spontaneous play at home was now resulting in his refusal to play without an adult; he was truly too scared to play. This required both Myla and Bruce to recognize that they tended to be more linear than spontaneous and that Dennis needed more spontaneous play with them.

This was tricky, but several sessions with the couple, without Dennis in the room, resulted in a good enough understanding to try something different. We managed to plan for a "spontaneous" experience; that is, all the planning occurred without Dennis's knowledge. Myla and Bruce arranged their work schedules so that they would have time to do something as a family. Going to the beach was suggested, and once there, they were to try to play. They could build sand castles, boogie board, or look for rocks, but they were to follow Dennis's lead. This meant no work talk, no planning of the next day, no cell phones, nothing but an afternoon at the beach as a family, and no nanny. It also meant not using a lot of words, not asking Dennis open-ended questions, like "what do you want to do tonight?" and not explaining why they were making a decision, unless Dennis asked them why, and then his parents would give only a brief response.

To Myla and Bruce's credit, once they understood the weight that words had on Dennis, they good-naturedly decided to monitor each other. I suggested they use a nonverbal signal in their monitoring. These were well-meaning parents who had not realized how their extremely verbal approach to life was affecting their son. It was only when I asked them how often Dennis laughs that it became clearer to them. Dennis doesn't really laugh, and they'd thought he was just a serious kid. He may be serious, but all kids laugh, even the most serious of four-year-olds. The beach outing was a success, and over time, such "spontaneous" family time increased.

Since Myla and Bruce said that Dennis had a friend, I encouraged them to consider playdates only at their house for a while with Bruce initially interacting in Dennis's play. I encouraged Bruce to avoid video games or TV but to interact with the children by following their lead and perhaps adding on to what they initiated. Bruce took to this well, and soon Myla did the same. Both parents clearly knew the goal was to increase Dennis's vitality, to make him laugh, and to increase his sense of security. This meant they had to do some hard soul-searching about their preoccupation with work. They did. They worked out a bit more flexibility in their week to include some regular family time together just for the three of them. Dennis, though initially hesitant, loved having his family to himself. He eventually was able to play with a friend with a parent in the background.

PLAY AND ATTACHMENT IN THE FOUR-YEAR-OLD

Four-year-olds can be very dramatic with big emotions that include a sense of outrage. They also like to have things their own way, and they can tattle. When four-year-old Clark's friend tried to put a pile of sand on Clark's sand castle, Clark was outraged and went immediately to his dad "to tell." Four-year-olds also like to show off what they can do and embellish stories that may sound like lies. They also can seem to tell lies, but sometimes their imagination gets the better of them, so parents have to be good at inquiring if a story is a "pretend" story or a "real" story. They will test rules and boundaries and can try to cover up mistakes. A child's reasoning is much stronger by four, and four-year-olds can't be fooled like they could at three. All in all, four-year-olds love play and conversation.

GAMES: Jokes, Questions, and Conversations

- Four-year-olds love to be asked questions that can show you that they know the answer. Having a conversation with your four-year-old about what he liked most about the day can be very interesting for him.

- He likes board games, matching games, putting puzzles together, and building with blocks or Legos.

- Going to the playground and climbing around on monkey bars and slides is immensely satisfying for him.

- He likes playing with balls, riding a tricycle (or maybe a bike with training wheels), or planting a garden.

- Reading stories together and asking him "what comes next?" lets him show you that he knows the story or allows him to create an imaginative story. Creating a story together using puppets is also fun for him.

- He will enjoy playing follow the leader or going on a form of scavenger hunt, such as "The first one who finds something blue wins." Let him then be a leader and see what he finds!

- You can make a collage of your four-year-old's favorite things by having him clip out pictures of what he likes from magazines and paste them onto construction paper.

- You can play the telephone game by whispering something in your child's ear and asking him to pass it on to the next person. This can be a hilarious game for a four-year-old.

PARENT FOCUS: HEALTH-CONSCIOUS PARENTS

Heather and Taylor were both working parents of three-year-old Nira and were expecting a second child in five months. They had both struggled with getting enough exercise even before Nira was born, and afterwards they found it even harder to fit in exercise, since they didn't like to spend time away from her. Now that Heather was pregnant, she wanted to start taking walks again, for walking made her feel better and it helped her relax. Taylor also wanted to make time to work out in the gym. Heather and Taylor decided to establish a one-hour time slot each night, which they would alternate using for exercise. On her night, Heather walked while Taylor started Nira's bedtime routine. On his night, Taylor went to the gym while Heather took over the bedtime routine. This way, both Heather and Taylor felt better about themselves.

LIVING IN THE CHARM: JACK'S CURIOSITY

Jack was an adorable four-year-old who heard his mother excitedly clapping and hollering "Hooray, Roger!" as she watched Roger Federer win his fifth Wimbledon tennis finals against Rafael Nadal. Jack, curious about why his mom was so excited, came in and asked, "Who's that guy?" His mother said that guy was named Roger and the other was named Rafael. Jack paused for a moment, looked at the TV screen, then looked back at his mother and asked, "Where are the other Ninja Turtles?"

CHAPTER 13

Baby On the Go

It does not hurt a baby to have to get to know someone new, especially if someone familiar can stay around while she does it. By tomorrow the stranger will seem less strange; if she is still there in a week or two she will be a known friend. But what if someone else is there tomorrow and someone else next week?
—Penelope Leach, *Children First*

A book about developing children under the age of five would not be complete without addressing the current controversy about child care. In the late 1970s and early 1980s, studies began to appear in the literature finding that nonmaternal care in the first year of life was associated with increased aggression in preschoolers. Other studies found that it wasn't so much having an infant in child care that was leading to later aggression but rather the cumulative effect of ongoing nonmaternal child care over the infant, toddler, and preschool developmental period that led to social-emotional problems (NICHD 2003). Still other studies not only found no negative effects from early child care but found positive effects (NICHD 2003). Then again, two studies using the Strange Situation found child care in infancy associated with insecure attachment, and in particular avoidant attachment (Vaughn, Deane, and Water 1985).

Given the dyadic nature of early development, along with the fact of more women in the workplace, a debate formed over the effect of non-maternal child care in the first year of life.

CHILD CARE RESEARCH

The National Institute of Child Health and Human Development (NICHD) responded to this concern by launching a study in the early 1990s, recruiting mothers after the birth of a child in ten different locations in the United States. This large study enrolled 1,364 one-month-old infants from diverse homes and began following their development. Multiple repeated interviews were given and measures taken over time, including the number of hours per week children were in child care, the age of child at entry, and the kind and quality of care. Mothers were the primary respondents, and maternal sensitivity was measured in the laboratory and at home over multiple time periods. Many other factors were monitored in this unique ongoing study, including family and child variables, like the mother's education, father or male partner in the home, family income, mother's depression (if any evident), and child's temperament and developmental skills. By three months, more than half the children in this study were in nonmaternal child care for an average of twenty-one hours a week, and by fifty-four months, behavioral problems were found in the children who had been in prolonged child care over the infant, toddler, and preschool developmental period, and this effect continued into kindergarten (NICHD 2003).

Of course, this created quite a stir and resulted in a subsequent analysis further investigating the size of this effect by comparing quantity, quality, and type of child care with parenting factors, including mother sensitivity. Interestingly, children in exclusive maternal care had mothers who tended to be more depressed, scored less on parent sensitivity, and had less income, while children from families with more income were in higher quality child care for more hours per week and had more center-based care (NICHD 2006). As reported in previous studies, however, the researchers continued to find that the quantity of child care was still associated with behavioral problems and poorer social skills at fifty-four months. They also found that increased hours in center-based child care, in particular, was associated with increased behavioral problems, although they also found increased hours associated with stronger cognitive and language skills (NICHD 2006).

The problem at this point was that although nonmaternal care included relative care, that is, an infant in the care of her father, grandmother, or other relative, such care was not sufficiently analyzed to see if it made a difference in the outcome. This is an especially important factor, for the Current Population Report on child care arrangements, surveyed during a four-month period in 2002, found that 63 percent of children under five were in child care; however, 40 percent were more likely cared for by a relative (Overturf Johnson 2005). In terms of our discussion in this book, fathers are viewed as primary caregivers, and relatives who have a unique investment in the child are viewed as a part of the "familiar" ongoing family context in a developing child's life. The burning question would be, then, are children in nonmaternal care but who are cared for by their own fathers and other relatives at greater risk for behavioral problems?

This was answered by the van IJzendoorn group (reported in Belsky et al. 2007), which reanalyzed the data and found that the association between quantity of child care and behavioral problems came specifically from time spent with nonrelatives (nannies, babysitters, day care homes, and center-based child care), and there was particularly a stronger association between center-based care and behavioral problems. The children have completed sixth grade now, and current analyses show three effects from ongoing early child care extending across the infant, toddler, and preschool developmental periods:

1. The quality of parenting predicted higher levels of social skills and positive social-emotional outcomes than did child care experience.

2. Children in higher quality center-based child care had higher vocabulary scores in fifth grade than children in lower quality center-based child care.

3. Children with more center-based child care, in particular, had more behavioral problems in sixth grade (Belsky et al. 2007).

Thus, the degree to which continuous child care is associated with behavioral problems (initially found in preschool children and maintained through the sixth grade) appears to be associated specifically with center-based child care (Belsky et al. 2007).

Now why would this be? Although future research will have to tackle this question, from an attachment and emotional regulation perspective, I could hazard a guess. The very young child is simply completely dependent on her caregivers to regulate her internal physiology. Another way to say this is that caregivers buffer the stress the child experiences, which is a direct correspondent to the child's developing nervous system. In very young childhood (birth to age three), a child's stress is regulated primarily by her parents. The question that leaps out is, how stressful is it for a young child in a child care setting without her parents? Vermeer and van IJzendoorn (2006) reviewed all studies investigating cortisol levels (stress hormone) taken in children in child care and found that children had higher cortisol levels in child care than they had in their own homes. They also found that this was especially true of children under thirty-six months of age. The level of stress, in particular, that a young child experiences in nonparental child care must be seriously studied and evaluated. Since child care centers, of course, have other children, they may be particularly stressful for children under three, whose developmental needs are still dyadic.

QUALITY OF CHILD CARE

It is clear to me that "quality of the child care" definitions need to include a greater understanding of right-brain regulatory development within the first three years of life. Children being cared for by nonrelatives need to be able to depend upon a caregiver as a secondary attachment figure whom they can rely on to understand and provide for what they need. It also means that the caregiver must be able to attune to the child's needs for stimulation and regulation accurately enough to establish a trusting relationship. Sir Richard Bowlby (John Bowlby's son) has recently written a position paper entitled "Stress in Daycare," in which he concluded that "babies and toddlers in daycare can avoid stress and anxiety if they have a secondary attachment figure who always looks after them" (Bowlby 2007, 1). I couldn't agree more, but the key word here is "always."

Child care centers, in particular, are fraught with turnover because of low-paying jobs; it's also money that determines whether or not the infant and toddler adult/child ratios can be lowered from the state-determined licensing requirements. In San Diego, our First 5 Commission (one of fifty-eight county commissions in California established through a tax on tobacco products) has funded for a number of years a program that reduces staff turnover. It does this by giving stipends to child care staff who pursue higher educational degrees in child development while staying employed on the same site for a required amount of time.

Developmentally, most three- and four-year-olds thrive in preschool, but parents need to be aware that the primary need of their infants and toddlers is a dyadic right-brain, relational, and social-emotional need, not a left-brain learning need. It is extremely important that child care given within the first three years of life is relational-based and informed by attachment and affect regulation theories. In my opinion, all staff caring for children under three need specific training based on the fact that they are functioning as secondary attachment figures for children; they should also have available to them ongoing consultations with developmental professionals trained in these two theories.

Certainly, I serve in this function for the St. Vincent's child care program, a program that is generally the first level of intervention we use for the young homeless child coming in from the streets. The structure and routines in the program, including toys and play, function as a regulatory experience for children who are generally quite dysregulated from their experiences prior to shelter. I meet with all child care staff and the program manager and supervisors on a biweekly basis to help them see children's regulation needs. I also suggest on-site plans, conversations with the parent, and other in-house interventions and assessments, or determine the need for outside referrals. This is a level of support for staff members who are working online in state-determined ratios of one adult to four infants and one adult to six toddlers. Their work is extremely demanding, requiring relational competence while performing the administrative duties required. Although this book has been written chiefly for parents, I hope it also will help those in the child care industry become more aware of the dyadic attunement needed to care for a child in the first three years of life.

But, of course, it doesn't stop at three. Any child who is in ongoing child care needs attunement and help with her emotional regulation;

thus, all child care staff members need ongoing support and training on attachment and emotional regulation. Child care staffs of school-age children also need this level of support, as also much can be done noninvasively on-site to help support emotional regulation in school-age children. I have been the consultant for a large after-school program in San Diego for close to eighteen years. This program, run by SAY San Diego Inc., provides after-school care for kindergarteners through sixth graders in a number of public schools in the San Diego School District. Monthly, I meet with the site supervisors and do training on child-development topics that are anchored in attachment and affect regulation theories. This is coupled with an on-site multisensory group called the Starshine Hour that serves as scaffolding for development. Much can be done on child care sites to support development, especially when staffs receive the relational support and tools they need.

We are in a time when neuroscience is overwhelmingly pointing to how emotional (dys)regulation affects brain development and future behavioral adjustment, and this quantity-of-child-care effect is not going away. In fact, Jacob (2007) critically reviewed the existing studies published between 1998 and 2006 on the association between nonmaternal child care and social-emotional development. Other than the NICHD studies, there were only five other studies available. Jacob pointed to the total lack of theory-driven hypotheses proposed to explain the association between nonmaternal care and social-emotional development. A good place to start would be with attachment theory and its critical role in affect regulation. We cannot continue to ignore the elephant in the room, even if we don't quite know how to get it out yet.

MORE OPTIONS ARE NEEDED

So where are we in all of this, and where does it leave parents? In therapy, I often encourage clients to at least hold on to what seems true in their minds, even if they don't know what to do about it and even if they have opposing thoughts and feelings, as over time, they will move toward a right-fitting solution. By holding all the child care issues in mind, I believe we can come up with solutions that truly serve children and their families. As we struggle with these issues as a society, we can't let go of some of the knowledge that we now have. The truths uncovered are as follows:

1. The first three years of life are critical for secure attachment and social-emotional development and regulation.

2. Children need sensitive, interactive, and attuned experiences that enhance positive feelings while regulating negative feelings.

3. The dyadic quality of the first three years of life has a direct correspondence to the healthy growth and maturation of the right hemisphere.

4. This base becomes the base from which all future development rests.

As a rule of thumb, when we don't know what to do, we need more information. This information should include the emotional needs of the parents, particularly the mother. In one of the NICHD studies reviewed by Jacob (2007), behavioral problems in children at thirty-six months were associated with the mother's attitude toward employment. That is, if a child was in full-time maternal care yet the mother had strong positive beliefs about employment, or, conversely, the mother was working but had strong positive beliefs about staying at home, that child was rated with more behavioral problems. To me, this is not rocket science, as most of us know that when a mother is unhappy, her unhappiness can affect not only her but her entire family, particularly her developing children. This clearly indicates that before parents make decisions about child care, mothers should pause long enough to honestly acknowledge their true feelings about returning to work.

Mothers who are financially able to stay at home with their young children may be able to get their adult-world needs met by volunteering in schools or other organizations of interest. Some stay-at-home mothers (or fathers) have home-based businesses that they run around their child's schedule. Other mothers elect to return to their careers, with parents juggling work and child care schedules as best they can. Some professional couples who have more control over their time can coordinate their schedules so one of them is with their young child, asking relatives to step in as needed. For many parents, though, especially single parents, the above options are generally not possible, as financial concerns are primary and quality child care an urgent necessity. Even though the NICHD sample included 24 percent ethnic minorities and 15 percent single mothers, the sample itself more reflects a white household with a median income and mothers with higher levels of education than average: that is, a low-risk population (Jacob 2007). It has certainly been my experience that high-quality center-based child care can actually be therapeutic and stabilizing for high-risk children.

Leaving your infant in the hands of another is often hard on mothers and can be hard for fathers too. Mothers who prefer to stay at home with their infants but cannot do so for financial reasons often long for their infants during the workday. Our powerful right-brain-to-right-brain inter-actions with our infants bond us, making it quite difficult to shift into the left-brain focus generally required by the workplace. And, of course, nature has a reason for this. Add to this that many women with children want to be able to continue to advance in their careers, and the question of child care in our time becomes a very complex issue. It seems to me that parents need more options available to them when considering how to care for their young children, particularly infants and toddlers.

FAMILY AND MEDICAL LEAVE ACT

In the United States, the Family and Medical Leave Act (FMLA) allows for twelve weeks of unpaid leave over a twelve-month period for child-birth, newborn care, adoption, or the care of an ill family member. This act protects the employee's job and benefits while on leave. However, the law covers companies only over a certain size, and to be eligible, employees must have worked a certain minimum amount of time. The International Labor Organization, a United Nations agency focused on worldwide labor standards, has encouraged all member nations to provide at least two-thirds pay for up to eighteen weeks for maternity leave, but still encourages nations to pay 100 percent of the employee's "usual" earnings if possible (Calnen 2007). Many countries have paid maternity leave. For example, in Norway, mothers can receive either 100 percent of their usual earnings for a forty-two week period or 80 percent of their earnings over a fifty-two week period; Italy has five months of paid leave, the United Kingdom fourteen weeks, and India twelve weeks

(Calnen 2007). Like the United States, Australia has no paid maternity leave but gives one-year job protection (Associated Press 2005). In the United States, fathers can also take unpaid leave within the stipulations of FMLA.

It's clear to me that we need to further explore the association of quantity of child care and behavioral problems, especially looking at center-based care. Without a doubt, we should begin by looking at how child care experiences differ based on how much attuned emotional regulation children receive, assuming they are with reliable caregivers who give them good physical care as well. What may turn out to play a significant role in the quality of child care is the ability of caregivers to enhance positive emotions. Children without a lot of positive emotional experiences at home indeed may do better on a high-quality child care site. But those who have ongoing and regular positive emotional experiences with their parents at home may not do so well. Given the realities of child care ratios, child care staffs have little time to sit and play with one baby for any prolonged time. Positive affect, or vitality affects, so important for infant development and secure attachment, take a bit of time in an ongoing, attuned relationship, and there may be large hidden differences in this factor for children in child care.

Overall, we need to give more thought and attention to the child care industry, given that child care staffs serve as secondary attachment figures for so many young children. Society needs to address this enormous responsibility. We are in need of policy changes to offer more support to parents with young children, especially those under three years of age. As a start, a solution worth exploring is providing parents with paid maternity and paternity leave, coupled with flextime employment options during the first three years of life and the availability of high-quality child care. Furthermore, child care staffs should receive special training and support for their important roles as secondary attachment figures. It would be a beginning.

IN PARTING: ATTACHEMENT MATTERS

We have come to the end of our time together, and I wish you and your family the best of living. I hope to have given you not only important information about attachment and its role in brain and social-emotional development and regulation, but also the confidence that you can raise your child well by knowing her through your own attunement to her. As you help her regulate her emotions and express interest and delight in her exploration and accomplishments, you show her that she matters. This is how children feel secure, and this is how they feel known.

References

Ainsworth, M. D. S. 1967. *Infancy in Uganda: Infant Care and the Growth of Love.* Baltimore, MD: Johns Hopkins University.

Ainsworth, M. D. S., M. C. Blehar, E. Waters, and S. Wall. 1978. *Patterns of Attachment: A Psychological Study of the Strange Situation.* Hillsdale, NJ: Erlbaum.

American Academy of Pediatrics. 2005. Policy statement. Breastfeeding and the use of human milk. *Pediatrics* 115(2):496–506.

Asher, I., B. Kaplan, I. Modai, A. Neri, A. Valevski, and A. Weizman. 1995. Mood and hormonal changes during late pregnancy and puerperium. *Clinical and Experimental Obstetrics and Gynecology* 22:321–325.

Associated Press. 2005. U.S. stands apart from other nations on maternity leave. *USA Today,* July 26.

Attia, E., J. Downey, and M. Oberman. 1999. Postpartum psychoses. In *Postpartum Mood Disorders,* edited by L. J. Miller. Washington, DC: American Psychiatric Press.

Balbernie, R. 2001. Circuits and circumstances: The neurobiological consequences of early relationship experiences and how they shape later behavior. *Journal of Child Psychotherapy* 27(3):237–255.

Beebe, B., and F. M. Lachmann. 2002. *Infant Research and Adult Treatment.* Hillsdale, NJ: Analytic Press.

Belsky, J. 1984. The determinants of parenting: A process model. *Child Development* 55:83–96.

————. 1999. Modern evolutionary theory and patterns of attachment. In *Handbook of Attachment: Theory, Research, and Clinical Applications,* edited by J. Cassidy and P. R. Shaver. New York: Guilford Press.

Belsky, J., D. L. Vandell, M. Burchinal, K. A. Clarke-Stewart, K. McCartney, M. T. Owen, and the NICHD Early Child Care Research Network. 2007. Are there long-term effects of early child care? *Child Development* 78(2):681–701.

Benoit, D., and K. C. H. Parker. 1994. Stability and transmission of attachment across three generations. *Child Development* 65:1444–1456.

Bokhorst, C. L., M. J. Bakermans-Kranenburg, P. M. Fearon, M. H. van IJzendoorn, P. Fonagy, and C. Schuengel. 2003. The importance of shared environment in mother-infant attachment security: A behavioral genetic study. *Child Development* 74:1769–1782.

Bowlby, J. 1952. *Maternal Care and Mental Health*. 2nd ed. Geneva: World Health Organization.

———. 1969/1982. *Attachment and Loss*. Vol. 1, *Attachment*. New York: Basic Books.

———. 1973. *Attachment and Loss*. Vol. 2, *Separation*. New York: Basic Books.

———. 1980. *Attachment and Loss*. Vol. 3, *Loss, Sadness and Depression*. New York: Basic Books.

———. 1988. *A Secure Base: Parent-Child Attachment and Healthy Human Development*. New York: Basic Books.

Bowlby, R. 2007. Babies and toddlers in non-parental daycare can avoid stress and anxiety if they develop a lasting secondary attachment bond with one carer who is consistently accessible to them. *Attachment & Human Development* 9(4):307–319.

Brazelton, T. B. 1992. *Touchpoints. Birth to 3*. New York: Perseus Publishing.

Calnen, G. 2007. Paid maternity leave and its impact on breastfeeding in the United States: A historic, economic, political, and social perspective. *Breastfeeding Medicine* 2(1):34–44.

Carlson, E. A. 1998. A prospective longitudinal study of attachment disorganization/disorientation. *Child Development* 69(4):1107–1128.

Carlson, V., D. Cicchetti, D. Barnett, and K. Braunwald. 1989. Disorganized/disoriented attachment relationships in maltreated infants. *Development Psychology* 25(4):525–531.

Carter, R. 1998. *Mapping the Mind.* Berkeley, CA: University of California Press.

Cassidy, J., and L. Berlin. 1994. The insecure/ambivalent pattern of attachment: Theory and research. *Child Development* 65:971–981.

Chiron, C., I. Jambaque, R. Nabbout, R. Lounes, A. Syrota, and O. Dulac. 1997. The right brain hemisphere is dominant in human infants. *Brain* 120:1057–1065.

Cox, M. J., M. Tresch Owen, J. M. Lewis, and V. K. Henderson. 1989. Marriage, adult adjustment, and early parenting. *Child Development* 60:1015–1024.

Cranley, M. S. 1981. Development of a tool for the measurement of maternal attachment during pregnancy. *Nursing Research* 30:281–284.

Damasio, A. 1999. *The Feeling of What Happens.* New York: Harcourt.

DeCasper, A. J., and W. P. Fifer. 1980. Of human bonding: Newborns prefer their mothers' voices. *Science* 208:1174–1176.

de Graaf-Peters, V. B., and M. Hadders-Algra. 2006. Ontogeny of the human central nervous system: What is happening when? *Early Human Development* 82:257–266.

Dewey, K. G. 2004. Impact of breastfeeding on maternal nutritional status. *Advances in Experimental Medicine and Biology* 554:91–100.

De Wolff, M. S., and M. H. van IJzendoorn. 1997. Sensitivity and attachment: A meta-analysis on parental antecedents of infant attachment. *Child Development* 68(4):571–591.

Feldman, R. 2000. Parents' convergence on sharing and marital satisfaction, father involvement, and parent-child relationship at the transition to parenthood. *Infant Mental Health Journal* 21(3):176–191.

———. 2003. Infant-mother and infant-father synchrony: The coregulation of positive arousal. *Infant Mental Health Journal* 24(1):1–23.

Feldman, S. S., S. C. Nash, and B. G. Aschenbrenner. 1983. Antecedents of fathering. *Child Development* 54:1628–1636.

Field, T. 1985. Attachment as psychobiological attunement: Being on the same wavelength. In *The Psychobiology of Attachment and Separation*, edited by M. Reite and T. Field. New York: Academic Press.

Field, T., M. Diego, J. Dieter, M. Hernandez-Reif, S. Schanberg, C. Kuhn, R. Yando, and D. Bendell. 2004. Prenatal depression effects on the fetus and the newborn. *Infant Behavior and Development* 27:216–229.

Fields, J. 2003. *Children's Living Arrangements and Characteristics: March 2002*. Current Population Reports, P20–547. Washington, DC: U.S. Bureau of the Census.

Fields, J., and L. M. Casper. 2001. *America's Families and Living Arrangements: March 2000*. Current Population Reports, P20–537. Washington, DC: U.S. Bureau of the Census.

Fifer, W. P., and C. M. Moon. 1995. The effects of fetal experience with sound. In *Fetal Development: A Psychobiological Perspective*, edited by J. P. Lecanuet, W. P. Fifer, N. A. Krasnegor, and W. P. Smotherman. Hillsdale, NJ: Erlbaum.

Fincham, F. D. 1998. Child development and marital relations. *Child Development* 69(2):543–574.

Fonagy, P., M. Steele, H. Steele, G. S. Moran, and A. C. Higgitt. 1991. The capacity for understanding mental states: The reflective self in parent and child and its significance for security of attachment. *Infant Mental Health Journal* 12(3):201–218.

Fraiberg, S., E. Adelson, and V. Shapiro. 1975. Ghosts in the nursery: A psychoanalytic approach to impaired infant-mother relationships. *Journal of the American Academy of Child Psychiatry* 14:1387–1422.

Galin, D., J. Johnstone, L. Nakell, and J. Herron. 1979. Development of the capacity for tactile information transfer between hemispheres in normal children. *Science* 204:1330–1332.

Gazzaniga, M. S. 1988. *Mind Matters. How Mind and Brain Interact to Create Our Conscious Lives*. Boston: Houghton Mifflin.

George, C., N. Kaplan, and M. Main. 1984, 1985, 1996. *Adult Attachment Interview.* Unpublished protocols, University of California, Berkeley.

Gunnar, M. R., and B. Donzella. 2002. Social regulation of the cortisol levels in early human development. *Psychoneuroendocrinology* 27:199–220.

Hesse, E. 1999. The adult attachment interview: Historical and current perspectives. In *Handbook of Attachment: Theory, Research, and Clinical Applications,* edited by J. Cassidy and P. R. Shaver. New York: Guilford Press.

Jacob, J. I. 2007. The socio-emotional effects of non-maternal childcare on children in the USA: A critical review of recent studies. *Early Child Development and Care.* iFirst Article DOI: 10.1080/03004430701292988.

Joseph, R., R. E. Gallagher, W. Holloway, and J. Kahn. 1984. Two brains, one child: Interhemispheric information transfer deficits and confabulatory responding in children aged 4, 7, 10. *Cortex* 20(3):317–331.

Kaplan, J. E., and E. Zaidel. 2001. Error monitoring in the hemispheres: The effect of lateralized feedback on lexical decision. *Cognition* 82:157–178.

Karen, R. 1998. *Becoming Attached.* New York: Oxford Press.

Karr-Morse, R., and M. S. Wiley. 1997. *Ghosts from the Nursery: Tracing the Roots of Violence.* New York: Atlantic Monthly Press.

Kennaway, D. J., G. E. Stamp, and F. C. Goble. 1992. Development of melatonin production in infants and the impact of prematurity. *Journal of Clinical Endocrinology and Metabolism* 75:367–369.

Lamott, A. 1993. *Operating Instructions: A Journal of My Son's First Year.* New York: Anchor Books.

Luciana, M., and C. A. Nelson. 1998. The functional emergence of prefrontally-guided working memory systems in four-to-eight-year-old children. *Neuropsychologia* 36(3):273–293.

Lukowski, A. F., S. A. Wiebe, J. C. Haight, T. DeBoer, C. A. Nelson, and P. J. Bauer. 2005. Forming a stable memory representation in the first year of life: Why imitation is more than child's play. *Developmental Science* 8(3):279–298.

Lundqvist, C., and K. G. Sabel. 2000. Brief report: The Brazelton Neonatal Behavioral Assessment Scale detects differences among newborn infants of optimal health. *Journal of Pediatric Psychology* 25(8):577–582.

Lutkenhaus, P., K. E. Grossmann, and K. Grossmann. 1985. Infant-mother attachment at twelve months and style of interaction with a stranger at the age of three years. *Child Development* 56:1538–1542.

Lyons-Ruth, K. 1996. Attachment relationships among children with aggressive behavior problems: The role of disorganized early attachment patterns. *Journal of Consulting and Clinical Psychology* 64(1):64–73.

Mahler, M. S., F. Pine, and A. Bergman. 1975. *The Psychological Birth of the Human Infant: Symbiosis and Individuation.* New York: Basic Books.

Main, M. 2000. The organized categories of infant, child, and adult attachment: Flexible vs. inflexible attention under attachment-related stress. *Journal of the American Psychoanalytic Association* 48(4):1055–1096.

Main, M., and E. Hesse. 1990. Parents' unresolved traumatic experiences are related to infant disorganized attachment status: Is frightened or frightening parental behavior the linking mechanism? In *Attachment in the Preschool Years*, edited by M. T. Greenberg, D. Cicchetti, and E. M. Cummings. Chicago: University of Chicago Press.

Main, M., E. Hesse, and N. Kaplan. 2005. Predictability of attachment behavior and representational processes at 1, 6, and 19 years of age. In *Attachment from Infancy to Adulthood: Lessons from the Longitudinal Studies*, edited by K. E. Grossmann, K. Grossmann, and E. Waters. New York: Guilford Press.

Main, M., and J. Solomon. 1990. Procedures for identifying infants as disorganized/disoriented during the Ainsworth Strange Situation. In *Attachment in the Preschool Years*, edited by M. T. Greenberg, D. Cicchetti, and E. M. Cummings. Chicago: University of Chicago Press.

Mancia, M. 2006. Implicit memory and early unrepressed unconscious: Their role in the therapeutic process. (How the neurosciences can contribute to psychoanalysis). *International Journal of Psychoanalysis* 87:83–103.

Matsuzawa, J., M. Matsui, T. Konishi, K. Nogucki, R. C. Gur, W. Bilker, and T. Miyawaki. 2001. Age-related volumetric changes of brain gray and white matter in healthy infants and children. *Cerebral Cortex* 11:335–342.

Miller, L. J., and M. Rukstalis. 1999. Beyond the "blues." Hypotheses about postpartum reactivity. In *Postpartum Mood Disorders*, edited by L. J. Miller. Washington, DC: American Psychiatric Press.

Mirmiran, M., J. H. Kok, K. Boer, and H. Wolf. 1992. Perinatal development of human circadian rhythms: Role of the fetal biological clock. *Neuroscience and Biobehavioral Reviews* 16:371–378.

Moore, D. S. 2001. *The Dependent Gene*. New York: Henry Holt.

Muller, M. E. 1993. Development of the Prenatal Attachment Inventory. *Western Journal of Nursing Research* 15:199–215.

Murray, L., and P. J. Cooper, eds. 1997. *Postpartum Depression and Child Development*. New York: Guilford Press.

NICHD Early Child Care Research Network. 2003. Does amount of time spent in child care predict socioemotional adjustment during the transition to kindergarten? *Child Development* 74(4):976–1005.

———. 2006. Child-care effect sizes for the NICHD study of early child care and youth development. *American Psychologist* 61(2):99–116.

O'Hara, M. W. 1997. The nature of postpartum depressive disorders. In *Postpartum Depression and Child Development*, edited by L. Murray and P. J. Cooper. New York: Guilford Press.

Overturf Johnson, J. 2005. *Who's Minding the Kids? Child Care Arrangements: Winter 2002*. Current Population Reports, P70–101. Washington, DC: U.S. Bureau of the Census.

Panksepp, J. 1998. *Affective Neuroscience: The Foundations of Human and Animal Emotions*. New York: Oxford University Press.

Pollack, W. 1998. *Real Boys*. New York: Henry Holt.

Pretorius, D. H., S. Gattu, E. K. Ji, K. Hollenbach, R. Newton, A. Hull, S. Carmona, D. D'Agostini, and T. R. Nelson. 2006. Preexamination and postexamination assessment of parental-fetal bonding in patients undergoing 3-/4-dimensional obstetric ultrasonography. *Journal of Ultrasound in Medicine* 25:1411–1421.

Rees, B. L. 1980. Measuring identification with the mothering role. *Research in Nursing and Health* 3:49–56.

Repacholi, B. M., and A. Gopnik. 1997. Early reasoning about desires: Evidence from 14- and 18-month-olds. *Development Psychology* 33(1):12–21.

Saxe, R., and A. Wexler. 2005. Making sense of another mind: The role of the right temporoparietal junction. *Neuropsychologia* 43:1391–1399.

Schore, A. N. 1994. *Affect Regulation and the Origin of the Self: The Neurobiology of Emotional Development.* Hillsdale, NJ: Erlbaum.

———. 1996. The experience-dependent maturation of a regulatory system in the orbital prefrontal cortex and the origin of developmental psychopathology. *Development and Psychopathology* 8:9–87.

———. 1997. Early organization of the nonlinear right brain and development of a predisposition to psychiatric disorders. *Development and Psychopathology* 9:595–631.

———. 2000. Attachment and the regulation of the right brain. *Attachment and Human Development* 2(1):23–47.

———. 2001a. Effects of a secure attachment relationship on right brain development, affect regulation, and infant mental health. *Infant Mental Health Journal* 22(1–2):7–66.

———. 2001b. The effects of early relational trauma on right brain development, affect regulation, and infant mental health. *Infant Mental Health Journal* 22(1–2):201–269.

———. 2002. Dysregulation of the right brain: A fundamental mechanism of traumatic attachment and the psychopathogenesis of posttraumatic stress disorder. *Australian and New Zealand Journal of Psychiatry* 36:9–30.

———. 2003. *Affect Dysregulation and Disorders of the Self.* New York: Norton.

———. 2006. Psychoanalytic research: Progress and process. Developmental affective neuroscience and clinical practice. *Psychologist-Psychoanalyst* 26(2):13–16.

Scott, K. D., P. H. Klaus, and M. H. Klaus. 1999. The obstetrical and postpartum benefits of continuous support during childbirth. *Journal of Women's Health and Gender-Based Medicine* 8(10):1257–1264.

Shapiro, A. F., J. M. Gottman, and S. Carrere. 2000. The baby and the marriage: Identifying factors that buffer against decline in marital satisfaction after the first baby arrives. *Journal of Family Psychology* 14(1):59–70.

Shieh, C., M. Kravitz, and H. Wang. 2001. What do we know about maternal-fetal attachment? *Kaohsiung Journal of Medical Sciences* 17:448–454.

Sieratzki, J. S., and B. Woll. 1996. Why do mothers cradle babies on their left? *Lancet* 347:1746–1748.

Spangler, G., and K. E. Grossmann. 1993. Biobehavioral organization in securely and insecurely attached infants. *Child Development* 64:1439–1450.

Spence, S., D. Shapiro, and E. Zaidel. 1996. The role of the right hemisphere in the physiological and cognitive components of emotional processing. *Psychophysiology* 33:112–122.

Sroufe, L. A., B. Egeland, E. A. Carlson, and W. A. Collins. 2005. *The Development of the Person: The Minnesota Study of Risk and Adaptation from Birth to Adulthood.* New York: Guilford Press.

Stern, D. 1985. *The Interpersonal World of the Infant: A View from Psychoanalysis and Development Psychology.* New York: Basic Books.

Stuss, D. T., and M. P. Alexander. 1999. Affectively burnt in: A proposed role of the right frontal lobe. In *Memory, Consciousness, and the Brain*, edited by E. Tulving. Philadelphia: Psychology Press.

Thatcher, R. W. 1994. Cyclic cortical reorganization. Origins of human cognitive development. In *Human Behavior and the Developing Brain,* edited by G. Dawson and K. W. Fischer. New York: Guilford Press.

————. 1997. Neuroimaging of cyclic cortical reorganization during human development. In *Developmental Neuroimaging: Mapping the Development of Brain and Behavior,* edited by R. W. Thatcher, G. Reid Lyon, J. Ramsey, and N. Krasnegor. San Diego: Academic Press.

Trevarthen, C. 1990. Growth and education of the hemispheres. In *Brain Circuits and Functions of the Mind: Essays in Honor of Roger W. Sperry,* edited by C. Trevarthen. Cambridge, UK: Cambridge University Press.

Tronick, E. 2006. Already set-up for trauma: Infants' coping with stress, memory, and autonomic reactivity. PowerPoint presentation at the fifth annual Cutting Edge conference, presented by UCLA and the Lifespan Learning Institute, Los Angeles.

————. 2007. *The Neurobehavioral and Social-Emotional Development of Infants and Children.* New York: Norton.

van IJzendoorn, M. H. 1995. Adult attachment representations, parental responsiveness, and infant attachment: A meta-analysis on the predictive validity of the Adult Attachment Interview. *Psychological Bulletin* 117(3):387–403.

van IJzendoorn, M. H., and M. J. Bakermans-Kranenburg. 1996. Attachment representations in mothers, fathers, adolescents, and clinical groups: A meta-analytic search for normative data. *Journal of Consulting and Clinical Psychology* 64(1):8–21.

van IJzendoorn, M. H., and M. S. De Wolff. 1997. In search of the absent father: Meta-analyses of infant-father attachment: A rejoinder to our discussants. *Child Development* 68(4):604–609.

van IJzendoorn, M. H., C. Schuengel, and M. J. Bakermans-Kranenburg. 1999. Disorganized attachment in early childhood: Meta-analysis of precursors, concomitants, and sequelae. *Development and Psychopathology* 11:225–249.

Vaugnh, B. E., K. E. Deane, and E. Water. 1985. The impact of out-of-home care on child-mother attachment quality: Another look at some enduring questions. In *Growing points of attachment theory and research. Monographs of the Society for Research in Child Development*, edited by I. Bretherton and E. Waters. 50(1-2):110–135.

Vermeer, H. J., and M. H. van IJzendoorn. 2006. Children's elevated cortisol levels at daycare: A review and meta-analysis. *Early Childhood Research Quarterly* 21:390–401.

Vygotsky, L. S. 1978. *Mind in Society*. Cambridge, MA: Harvard University Press.

Weinfield, N. S., L. A. Sroufe, B. Egeland, and E. A. Carlson. 1999. The nature of individual differences in infant-caregiver attachment. In *Handbook of Attachment: Theory, Research, and Clinical Applications*, edited by J. Cassidy and P. R. Shaver. New York: Guilford Press.

Winnicott, D. W. 1965. *The Maturational Processes and the Facilitating Environment: Studies in the Theory of Emotional Development*. Madison, CT: International Universities Press.

Zelenko, M., H. Kraemer, L. Huffman, M. Gschwendt, N. Pageler, and H. Steiner. 2005. Heart rate correlates of attachment status in young mothers and their infants. *Journal of the American Academy of Child and Adolescent Psychiatry* 44(5):470–476.

Aquario Studio

Ruth P. Newton, Ph.D., is a licensed clinical psychologist specializing in attachment and affect regulation in the developing child. She is also the supervising psychologist for Child and Mental Health Services at St. Vincent de Paul Village, a homeless rehabilitation center in downtown San Diego, and a training supervisor for master and doctoral-level interns. Newton is on the advisory board for the Attachment Institute at the University of California, San Diego, and is a member of the Technical and Professional Advisory Committee for the First 5 Commission of San Diego, an organization that funds programming for children five years of age and younger and their families. She works with children and adults in a private practice in La Jolla, CA, and is a longtime consultant for SAY San Diego's Extended Day Childcare program. She is a contributing author to *Reader's Guide to Affect Regulation and Neurobiology* and *Play Therapy for Very Young Children.*